Typhoon Tale

JAMES KYLE D.F.M.

Fighter and Dive Bomber Pilot
Qualified Flying Instructor
Instrument Rating Examiner
Pilot/Navigator Instructor
Air Traffic Control Examiner

D1492785

GEORGE MANN *of* MAIDSTONE

TYPHOON TALE
by James Kyle D.F.M.

First published 1989
Fifth revised edition 2001

British Library Cataloguing in Publication Data.
A catalogue record for this book is available from the
British Library.

Library of Congress Cataloguing in Publication Data
applied for.

ISBN 07041 0306 0

Cover illustrations:
*Front — James Kyle in his Typhoon IB JP 682
of 197 Squadron approaching the Beachhead over
Landing Craft
at 0640 hrs on D-Day 6th June 1944* ·
(from a painting by Military Artist John Batchelor.)

Back — the Author in 1946.

Printed and bound in Great Britain and published by
George Mann Books, PO Box 22, Maidstone ME14 1AH
in the English County of Kent

Dedicated to my family: Denise, David and Jamie

Complete family Malta 1962

'An Appointment in Samarra'

There was a merchant in Bagdad who sent his servant to market to buy provisions, and in a little while the servant came back, white and trembling, and said, "Master, just now when I was in the market-place I was jostled by a woman in the crowd and when I turned I saw it was Death that jostled me. She looked at me and made a threatening gesture; now, lend me your horse, and I will ride away from the city and avoid my fate. I will go to Samarra and there Death will not find me." The merchant lent him his horse and the servant mounted it, and he dug his spurs in its flanks and as fast as the horse could gallop he went. Then the merchant went down to the market-place and he saw Death standing in the crowd and he came to Death and said, "Why did you make a threatening gesture to my servant when you saw him this morning?" "That was not a threatening gesture," Death said. "It was only a start of surprise. I was astonished to see him in Bagdad, for I had an appointment with him tonight in Samarra."

Contents

Acknowledgements

The author wishes to acknowledge with thanks the Controller of Her Majesty's Stationery Office for permission to reproduce the brief extracts from *Royal Air Force 1939-45, vol. 1: The Fight at Odds.*

Acknowledgement is given to the Royal Air Force Museum, Hendon, and the Imperial War Museum for permission to reproduce photographs (on pages 77, 105, 121, 131, 132 and 178), and to others for a few apposite facts and phrases of the era.

A sincere thanks to my good friend Eric H. Day for his watercolour painting presented to me some twenty years ago and to John Batchelor for his superb painting of my D-Day story.

Many thanks also to Chris Thomas for his thoughtful and splendid foreword, and to Curtis M. Penland for his help and deep interest in my story.

To my son David for his ballad 'All the Young Airmen'.

Foreword

James Kyle's story centres around his operational 'tour' flying the mighty Hawker Typhoon – a British interceptor and ground-attack aircraft that enjoyed a brief but spectacular career within the span of the war years and then, undeservedly, faded into relative obscurity.

From the same stable that produced such thoroughbreds as the Sopwith Camel (the most successful British fighter of the First World War) and the graceful Hawker Fury of the thirties, the Typhoon was conceived, in 1937, as the successor to the Hurricane, yet to become the RAF's most prolific interceptor in the Battle of Britain. It was to be powered by an advanced in-line piston engine, the Napier Sabre, which promised to deliver more than 2,000 hp – twice the power of the then current Hurricane. First flown in early 1940, development was delayed by the more urgent priorities of the Battle of Britain, and by problems with the twenty-four-cylinder, twin crankshaft, sleeve-valved Sabre. It was not until September 1941 that Typhoons, the RAF's first aircraft capable of more than 400 mph, were delivered to an eager Fighter Command.

However, despite an electrifying turn of speed at low level, the Typhoon proved disappointing in its envisaged role of interceptor, as performance above 15,000 feet was inferior to that of the Spitfires it was scheduled to replace. Problems for the Typhoon mounted, as the highly complex Sabre continued to give trouble and, just as the Typhoon became operational in mid-1942, a serious airframe fault became evident. Growing numbers of Typhoons shed their complete tail assemblies in flight, almost invariably with fatal results for their pilots.

Early in 1943 cancellation of the entire Typhoon programme seemed unavoidable, but this was averted thanks, in the main, to two factors. The first of these was the increased frequency of German fighter-bomber attacks on English south coast targets. The Typhoon was the only weapon available to Fighter Command to counter these intruders, which crossed the Channel at high speed and below radar cover. Secondly, it was realized that the low level performance of the Typhoon, combined with the fixed armament of four 20 mm cannons, steadiness as a gun platform and load carrying ability, rendered it the ideal fighter-bomber.

Success followed success in both these roles and by the autumn of 1943 more than sixty German raiders, two-thirds of them much-vaunted FW 190s, had been brought down. No fewer than eighteen squadrons of Typhoons were operating, mostly as fighter-bombers. By this time the major engine problems had been overcome and the incidence of tail failures was much reduced. Accordingly, the Typhoon was chosen as the premier ground-attack aircraft for the 2nd Tactical Air Force, which was then being formed to provide air support for the British and Canadian Armies in the forthcoming invasion of Europe.

On D-Day the RAF and RCAF fielded twenty squadrons of Typhoons, some of which were among the first over the beach-head. In the following weeks they played a vital role in the battle for Normandy, establishing a well-earned reputation for fast and accurate close support, with bombs or rockets. German supplies and reinforcements were constantly hindered by interdiction missions. Typhoons also carried out a series of highly successful 'pin-point' attacks on German Army headquarters, in which many staff officers, including Generals, were killed. On 7 August 1944 Typhoons played the major role in the battle of Mortain, when German armoured thrusts which threatened to split the Allied forces in Normandy, were halted and then savaged by incessant air attack. This pattern was continued across Belgium, Holland, into Germany and finally to victory. Within five months of VE Day the Typhoon had been withdrawn from frontline service, its place taken by the Hawker Tempest, a development of the Typhoon that had entered the fray in the last year of the war. It was the Allies' most effective medium and low level fighter aircraft.

After a short spell in storage most of the remaining Typhoons were scrapped in 1947; all had gone from the UK by the end of 1955. Fortunately one example had gone to the USA for trials in 1944, and had eventually come under the protection of the Smithsonian Institute. Thanks to the Institute's generosity, this sole survivor of 3,317 built, now resides in the RAF Museum at Hendon. The achievements of the aircraft were, of course, the achievements of the pilots and more than 600 of those young men paid the ultimate price for their endeavours. James Kyle must count himself fortunate to be among the survivors – for of those who joined 197 Squadron on its formation late in 1942, precious few completed a full tour of operations. In his book he has provided the reader with rather more than just the anticipated thrills of fighter sorties. Like many of his generation the Second World War changed his life completely and he reveals with candour and humour his progress from an underprivileged Scottish boyhood, through the rigours and demands of pilot training, to the harsh realities of life as a fighter-bomber pilot. A real 'Typhoon Tale'.

Chris Thomas (co-author of *Typhoon and Tempest Story*)

CHAPTER 1

In a Playground of Poverty

No pleasures like the skirl of the pipes, the flash of the sporran, salmon fishing or the stalking of the deer ever entered my poor Scottish existence. Like those around us we lived a penurious life, for I was an only child in a mining village in the 1920s. Grinding, grim poverty and deprivation existed in abundance throughout the country. The general strike of 1926 played its part in the squalor and spartan life of the working classes.

The village, situated on the banks of the River Clyde on the south-western outskirts of Motherwell (and subsequently destroyed) consisted of three rows of two bedroom cottages, without baths, forty-four to a row, each with an adjoining outside flush toilet. There were few shops. Four wash houses set equidistant between each row were booked for half a day once a week, but never on a Sunday, for the family wash. Most cottages were cold, clean but sparsely furnished and palely lit by gaslight; a single connection hung from the middle of the ceiling which emitted a feeble flickering light. We could see the pitshafts from the cottages and, beyond them, penetrating the horizon, the rounded tips of the numerous slag heaps.

My father, James, died in 1932 when I was ten years old. I was pulled out of the classroom while participating in mock eleven plus examinations to witness this mysterious thing called death. His face was colourless and sunken as he lay on the bed. He looked asleep, but when I touched him he felt cold. I moved quickly away, disturbed, and crept quietly outside to hide my feelings. I had never seen death before. When I returned inside they were moving him on to the table in the cold back room.

He was a foreman of the mines and had taken me down the local pits, all three of them, to the coalface. I found it thrilling as a small boy to fit the pilot light on my trouser belt and be issued with a torch before descending in the lift with the men. The drop down the pit shaft was awesome and the long walk underground to the coalface, passing men hard at work, avoiding the wagons and the ponies and the water pouring from the roof, made those excursions really fascinating. As I walked along beside him I was aware of the noise, the darkness and the polluted air in places, where the miners worked under claustrophobic cramped conditions. Even the Davy lamps and torches we carried could scarcely pierce the clouds of coal dust that were flung up at times. Most miners hacked away with a small hand drill, or pick and shovel. Machinery at the coalface was less than adequate.

At weekends we would encounter miners teeming out of the pits on their way home, bent and leaning forward, their faces black and eyes staring into the light of a new day. We knew them well but couldn't tell one from the other until they spoke to us. They had just completed the early shift of about ten hours for approximately 10s, all on pieces of bread and cheese or jam or bacon, and were arriving home to not much more. They surely must have thought the deal they got from life was a poor one. Seldom did they show their grievances and were usually quite jovial to us kids as we passed them by. None of them lived to see the days of the affluent miner.

The many pit ponies at work down the mines, poor things, were cocooned there for fifty weeks of the year. When let up for their annual holiday in the nearby pit fields they went berserk with delight. Running and charging round like mad, kicking, bucking and jumping like wild animals. We thought they might do themselves a mischief dashing madly towards the barbed wire fences at such high speeds. Children would go chasing after them. Older boys attempted to ride them bareback but very few succeeded. It was sad to see them all rounded up and sent back down the mines for yet another year.

I was also taken at infrequent intervals to the noisy and busy local barrow market in nearby Glasgow, that 'No Mean City'. These visits were a luxury for me – the drive on the bus, the stroll through the busy market-place which abounded with china, clothing, carpets, pictures, bedding, fruit and vegetables, kitchen items, antiques and old junk on a multitude of stalls. We would wander for hours through the lines of crowded stalls and shoppers. It gave me an exciting feeling. I would be impressed at my father's techniques and astuteness in bargaining with the embryo entrepreneurs. Biding his time for a particular article, he would argue the point and eventually, after some weeks if necessary, would succeed in purchasing the article at the price he was originally willing to pay. I admired him for his conviction, wondering how he always managed to succeed in these transactions. While we were in Glasgow a trip on the trams was always welcome. The special treat was to stare at the pulley sparking on the overhead wires; always a fascination.

When I was seven years old, I set out on a Sunday morning early with my father and our old pekinese dog, which had been in the family twice as long as me. My father and I made conversation as we strolled for miles along the highways and byways, across lush green fields and along tree-lined lanes, until we came to a large reservoir. We stopped and looked at the stretch of deep water. My father then turned to me and said:

'Jim, would you care to look around and find me a good sized brick or large stone?' Dutifully I scooted around, searching the area until I found what he wanted.

When I handed it to him, I was aghast and horrified at his immediate actions, because, before I realized what was happening, the pekinese was in the water with the brick tied round its neck. The poor beast was sinking fast. Father had managed to do the dirty deed so very quickly. There was nothing I could have done to stop him, even if I had been aware of his intentions. It was all so totally unexpected. I was shocked beyond belief. I stared at him, shouting hate at my father for being so cruel. I cried on and off all the way home.

He explained as we took the long road back that the dog was very old and had gone blind; this was his only means of putting the poor creature out of its misery. He said he was unable to pay the fees for the dog to be 'done' properly. This, however, was no consolation for me as I sobbed along beside him. I was very sad for a long time over the whole episode. It's been my predilection since never ever to be a dog owner. I considered it wouldn't be prudent to bear the traumatic experience again, so any affinity I had with dogs ended that sad Sunday morning.

At the age of eight, a small boy with dark hair and blue eyes, I was rushed to hospital one evening with a virulent attack of scarlet fever. It was to be the first and only illness that took me away from home overnight. I was frightened and apprehensive as they carried me away in the ambulance.

To my great alarm, they opened up a large new ward to put me in and, after only a few minutes, they switched off the light and left me in the room all by myself. It was dark and lonely in the vastness of the ward, with ominous darker rooms just discernible, their entrances showing at the far end. It was the first time I had been alone. I was still having childish nightmares and was really scared as I cowered into my pillow. Left lying alone in this strange bed with my fears, it wasn't long before I was shouting and screaming and making such a din that the nurses eventually had to come hurrying to switch on the lights. I told them of my predicament in a fearful manner, so they gave me the company of another small boy taken from another ward, and put him in the bed next to mine. His name was Archie Steel. He had blond hair and a fair peach-like complexion with pale blue eyes. We became great friends immediately. His presence in the huge ward was all that I needed to ward off the fear of that first night in hospital.

We had great fun talking at length, playing games and singing when we were happy. He taught me the words of a tune called 'The Highlander' which started with the words: 'Let me think of the days that are gone, Maggie, when you and I were young.' We sang it often late into the evening long after lights out. I recall cavorting about one day having one of our many pillow fights together, when I lost my balance, fell out of bed and dislocated my left arm. I remember looking at it in surprise as it appeared an awkward shape, was twisted and some inches shorter than my other one. But it was soon to be repaired by an appropriate tug from the doctor. I believe my stay in hospital lasted about three weeks and I felt I had thoroughly enjoyed myself.

My first trip to the public baths at the age of nine was a disaster. I was forcefully persuaded to go there by some teenagers who were competent swimmers. Soon after we had changed into our costumes, without warning I was manhandled by my companions and thrown into the pool at the deep end. I couldn't swim and I was unlikely to get any assistance from my so-called friends. It was panic stations as I hit the water and sank below. I struggled and spluttered to the top for the first time, gasping for breath. Flaying the water and kicking madly I made adequate movement above and below the surface to enable me to make headway towards the side and firmly grasp the rounded protrusions at the edge of the pool. I was paralysed with fear of drowning. Terror loaned me desperate strength and no human force could have dislodged my hands from the grip I had on the side fittings. Of course a number of helpfuls tried, not knowing how scared I was to let go.

It took years for me to enter a swimming pool again. I eventually had to, when I obtained an 'X' swimming certificate for aircrew while training to become a pilot during the Second World War. This culminated in jumping from a helicopter into the English Channel.

The leader of our gang was the eldest, the tallest and the strongest. His deputy, or so he thought he was, was a bit of a bully and a provocative character who tended to tease me more than the others. He tantalizingly tormented me for nigh on two years and I was a little afraid of him. One day he went too far and I was forced to fight him. I hit him with all the force I could muster and he fell to the ground, his face covered in blood. I fell on top of him and kept bashing away at his face and thumping him all over until he gave up the battle with a protracted strangled shout. I had surprised myself at the thrashing I handed out. The punitive measures I had inflicted on him were still visible, though not conspicuous, some days later. So the bullying stopped and the long period of attrition was over. We were to be close friends afterwards.

I was caught pinching pears when I was ten years old and had just passed my eleven plus examination. Having just left the primary school, three of us decided to rob the headmaster's garden, which was adjacent to the school playground. He had some lovely rich apple and pear trees, burdened with fruit and just over and close to the fairly high wall at the bottom of his garden. We approached under cover towards the rear of the house in the late afternoon. I went forward to reconnoitre, reported that all was clear, so was lifted up and slipped quickly over the wall. Dropping some 6 ft, and quickly scrambling up the tree, I was busy plundering, both pockets full and my jumper loaded, when quite unexpectedly from below a hand grabbed my ankle and a voice bellowed up:

'What in hell are you doing up there?' I looked down to see it was the headmaster and literally wet myself with fright.

Angrily he pulled me down, not letting go of me. He then proceeded to twist my arm high up behind my back until it hurt. In this fashion he marched me out through his front gate and along the main thoroughfare towards the police station half a mile away. As we moved along the road I noticed a gang of men, the corner roughs of the district, lounging across the other side of the road at the local pub. I pretended to be in real pain. Crying and shouting out loud that the headmaster was hurting me and twisting my arm, it attracted their attention. 'What are you doing to the kid?' they called. I cried even louder. The men sallied across the road towards us and approached the headmaster.

'Why are you hurting the boy?' they demanded in not very quiescent terms. After some menacing gestures and further expletives about inexcusably torturing a small boy, they demanded that I should be loosed at once. The headmaster was forced to let me go.

I ran like hell, found some sanctuary in the long grass and got rid of all my hidden loot in a nearby nettle patch, then made off home. Shaking a little and incoherent as I arrived indoors my mother could tell there was something wrong but she never closely questioned me. Some days later, as the police had not called at the house as expected, I sneaked back to the nettle patch and collected the pears which by now were lovely, sweet and ripe; I ate them all. The rest of the gang never asked whether or not I had managed to get any pears. They were only too glad not to have become involved.

At mid-morning my father died. He had been fifty-nine a few days before they buried him. Very few people came and I was not allowed to attend the funeral. He died from a tumour in the chest created by a kick from the back end of a pit pony. I was reminded of him during the Second World War when looking at a photograph of General Wavell.

My mother, Mary, died four years after my father. I was then fourteen and alone. I cannot remember too much about her. She was always quiet and unresponsive, and there was not much laughter or conversation between us. She was a considerate person and I don't recall any physical chastisement or ill treatment during my childhood even though she had ample reasons. Coping with my tantrums, idiosyncrasies and childish pranks needed patience. I remember tossing a brick through our window, flooding the floor of our cottage, destroying parts of the garden and refusing to run errands. I must have been a troublesome belligerent child, retaliating at the least opportunity if I didn't get my own way. And still I wasn't beaten or punished for my transgressions. Her great cure for all my ills was a large spoonful of castor oil or cascara. Like advice, they were easy to give but hard to take. How I hated them both.

Later in life she suffered physical disabilities that caused her much pain and inconvenience. I believe she developed diabetes which accelerated her death and she succumbed after a protracted debilitating troublesome period. She became unhappily distant and withdrawn, and was busy looking after

James Kyle, aged seven at
Motherwell, Scotland, in
1930, with his guardian

her illness. That made me unusually independent, as I had to care for myself; it may also have retarded my early development at a crucial stage. It took a long while to grow up. I felt little remorse and didn't cry at her demise. Her death left me stranded with no money, no family heirlooms, not even a photograph of my parents. She left nothing to remember either of them by. They both simply disappeared from earth. I was placed with a guardian.

The paucity of food and toys became evident as we village children got older. The food available was permanently plain and the meals were not always wholesome. So frugally did we eat that some of us developed rickets at an early age, and at times would be caught picking and eating cement from between wall bricks, unknowingly obtaining the calcium the body needed. Bread, potatoes, soups and stews were the bulk items; meat was too expensive. With little fresh fruit, diet was one of excess carbohydrates and paltry proteins.

Toys consisted mainly of secondhand bicycles, air rifles, meccano sets, packs of cards and bags of brightly coloured marbles. Birthday presents and parties were non-existent. Christmas was another negative. No decorations, holly or mistletoe adorned the rooms and Santa Claus was barely mentioned. Hanging up a stocking at the fireplace in the evening, collecting an apple, an orange, a few sweets and a nut or two, such was Christmas. We never knew the enchantment of the Christmas spirit that prevailed throughout the land. Nowadays, the annual ritual of over indulgence is seemingly more pagan than Christian.

There were precious few books around, no newspapers and very little other reading matter. No one wrote letters and the local library was distant, aloof and almost unknown to us. Conversation was limited and any mention of religion, education, politics or sex was in the most platitudinous terms. No educational stimuli existed. A few comics and books became available. The famous popular boys' magazines of the era like the *Wizard, Hotspur* and the *Rover* were readily exchanged, but we were in our teens before being able to obtain so-called adult reading material. These were short science fiction stories or sadistic semi-sexy detective paperbacks: the notorious *No Orchids for Miss Blandish* springs to mind. The struggle to get reading material was insurmountable and most of us developed an aversion to reading; this lack of opportunity drove us to the many games to be played outdoors. We were never avid readers.

Only from hindsight and with regret did I discover the consequences and grave errors I had made. The importance of books at that impressionable age was not perceived by me. It remains my predominant regret over the years.

Only once, at the age of nine, had I been taken away on holiday from this bleak environment, for a short cruise to Lochranza on the Isle of Arran. We sailed on a paddle steamer up the Clyde and subsequently from the town of Largs on the Ayrshire coast. It was the first time I had been aboard a train or boat and so very far from home. I was mesmerized by the feel of it all. The Isle of Arran was beautiful to me. A green paradise with lots of open space, bumble bees and butterflies, mountains and small clear rippling streams. I remember the flowers, the thick evergreen foliage and the profusion of ferns on the hillside, some of which were taller than I, as I became uncertain of my position when I climbed to the tops daily. It was indeed splendid to climb steep green hills to the highest peaks and enjoy at the top the warm embrace of sunlight on my upturned face. That week of inexpressible delight flashed away and soon it was time to return home. The one and only holiday remained a high point of ecstasy in a rather drab young life.

Special events or red letter days were few and far between. The first came at the Sunday School outing, when we played ourselves to a standstill and came home tired and exhausted; it was followed in the school summer holidays by the Glasgow Fair. There the introduction of the Big Wheel or Dipper meant we went higher than we had ever been before. Then there was 'Halloween' when we went 'dookin' for apples and finally Hogmanay, the great festival of Scotland, most awaited and loved by many. On the stroke of midnight when the church bells pealed, and the steak pie was brought from the hot oven, we sang 'Auld Lang Syne' and finally went 'first footing' in the falling snow. My atavistic impulses were always ready when this very Scottish commemoration was celebrated throughout my travels later in life.

We were a mischievous gang of six, ages ranging from nine to twelve, and we were to remain together as a gang for almost five years. The dissolution came at the ending of our school days and the start of work. There was nothing to keep us indoors, and in my fallacious memory, it was always sunny and warm. We had no expensive toys to play with, nor did we need them. There was no radio in most houses and television was unheard of. We were poor in material things but unaware of it. So we had a great deal of fun living a vigorous and extremely active outdoor life with a prodigious facility for sheer devilment that gave us a great deal of pleasure in all our games.

Our days were full, playing around in desultory fashion, but our antics seldom shocked or caused serious trouble. We roamed the countryside getting into all sorts of mischief, and possibly only a lack of opportunity, or fear, or the possible consequences saved us from total delinquency. The village roads and country lanes, woods and fields were our playground. We were never idle, playing hard and competitively and enjoying ourselves from early morning until late into the evenings. I remember playing street football in the dusk many times, sometimes it got so dark one could barely see the ball. During those dark evenings we would occasionally glimpse a shooting star or meteorite as it sped across the heavens. We would take time off to stop and stare as it streaked in a shallow dive and disappeared towards the horizon.

With a minimum of animosity we played many team games, and innumerable ball games where there were plenty of hard knocks. Each of us aggressively competed and blatantly wanted to win and be top. Strength and tenacity were of considerable advantage. There was one game where we would head a large ball against the wall hundreds of times till we ended up with a swollen forehead and a stiff neck. We played rowdy games of cowboys and indians much to the annoyance of many adults. We played with tin cans, bows and arrows, slings and swings, flew kites, plunked marbles and amused ourselves with home-made toys. Some of us had wooden boxes fitted with old pram wheels and went careering full tilt down the old slag heaps or nearby steep slopes. With girds and cleeks we would run for miles enjoying every moment, being light of foot with or without our summer shoes. A gird was an iron hoop and a cleek its guide. We had pea-shooters, pop-guns, water pistols, yo-yos. Peevers and peeries were other sources of enjoyment. With a whip, the peeries (pear-shaped spinning tops spun by string) were kept spinning for hours. Peevers were flat round stones about 2½ inches in diameter.

The game of marbles, like all our games, was intense and highly competitive. If you were a good 'plunker', you could acquire a large collection. In plunking, you placed the highly streaked coloured marble between the knuckle of the bent thumb and forefinger then flicked the thumb to make the shot, attempting to hit the opponent's marble. I was a good and accurate plunker and won a substantial number of brightly coloured marbles. A heavy bagful was carried from game to game.

Some of us kept pigeons, a few even entered races. Others went bird nesting, collecting eggs from each nest then swapping their findings with others to make up sets. We fought and scrambled, diving for pennies thrown away at weddings. We blew up live frogs with strong grass straws. We played endless games of leap frog and gave pick-a-back rides, boisterously crashing hard to knock each other down. We made 'purns' out of empty wooden cotton reels notched at the ends, wrapped a piece of string around the reels and ripped them along people's window panes in the dark, creating a terrible rickety noise, then ran off. When the door opened there was no one to be seen, but we were watching from afar.

From our den in the woods, a little hut covered in branches and bracken, we poached small game along with some men who came with ferrets and snares. We operated with catapults, bows and arrows, slings and string, which were not very effective and caught little, but it was interesting to wait and watch with the men who came poaching. Having dug for worms we would indulge in unauthorized fishing with our primitive equipment. Our fishing spot was a small arched bridge by a waterfall on a tributary of the River Clyde where it was rumoured that Mary Queen of Scots once hid overnight from the henchmen of her cousin Elizabeth. The iron hook hanging under the centre of the arch was there for all to see. We caught few fish.

Our gang, with many other children, would join the procession and the marches of the Orange Walk held annually on 12 July to celebrate the victory of the Protestants of the Orange Order over the Roman Catholics and King James II hundreds of years before. We walked with the bands, shouting and singing their slogans and songs of 'No Surrender', 'The Sash' and 'King Billy Slew the dirty Fenian Crew', among others, which were noisily drummed out over the long march through the streets. We enjoyed the fervour of these 'Battle of the Boyne' anti-Roman Catholic celebrations. It was exciting and colourful. We were all Protestants but none of us or our families belonged to the fierce Orange Lodge Organization.

Only on one occasion did I get to see the famous or infamous Rangers versus Celtic football match at Hampden Park, Glasgow. I was positioned behind and to the right of the goal mouth. Soon after the game began the Celtic centre forward shot the ball hard at goal, missed, and hit me smack in the face – knocking my school cap off and landing it four rows back. The stinging in my face remained an irritant for the remainder of the game. At the end of the match it was another of those days when religion raised its ugly head and fighting broke out in the streets. 'Follow, follow, we will follow Rangers, everywhere, anywhere, we will follow on' was sung in unison and could be heard all over Sauchiehall Street. 'There's not a team like the Glasgow Rangers, no not one, no not one' was another song heard in the distance as the bus left the city. I was glad to get home.

We went by 'shank's pony' everywhere. We walked with untiring energy to school, Sunday school, church, the swimming pool, the cinema and football matches. We ran races for any reason, running miles either for pleasure or going messages (errands), usually for no reward, but sometimes to receive a pork pie, hot and oozing with juice and jelly, was marvellous.

We were perpetually hungry with all this exercise. Some of us were physically undernouished and ill-equipped to cope with all this hard running about. To supplement what food we got at home, we managed to find a variety of edibles from farmers' fields, hedgerows and local gardens. We trespassed at will. The farmers' fields were robbed of swedes, turnips, cabbages, carrots and potatoes. We roasted the potatoes in a wood fire, peeling off most of the burned black skin and sinking our teeth into the delicious steaming soft inside. Berries would be obtained from the hedges and rhubarb from the local gardens. We carried a small bag of sugar when out after the rhubarb, and dipped the rhubarb in this with every bite; it was delicious.

The local general store and other little shops in the poor back streets of Motherwell were another source of food and many of the owners may have found their profits dwindling every now and again. Those little shops with their grubby little windows displayed a variety of sweets, chewing gum, comics, packets of fags and many other inviting knick-knacks. Similar items and other odds and ends were lying loose on show on the counter inside and were easy prey for nimble fingers. These were some of the ways we overcame our hunger when the cupboards at home were bare.

In the dark, cold and wet winter evenings when the snow lay four feet thick outside and all outdoor play was impossible, I would visit the old couple next door. I felt at home the minute I crossed the threshold. He was of sallow complexion with an inch long scar below the right cheek bone, and a raconteur if ever there was one. He was a relatively new neighbour and had come down from the north of Scotland after a pit accident. He was not in good health.

I recall with nostalgic pleasure the nights with him and his wife. They had no children. He puffed at his clay pipe, which he kept on the edge of the mantelpiece; she knitted, looking down at her work but listening, and I sat on the rug at his feet. I had adopted this man as my surrogate father until he too died. He really meant a great deal to me when I was ten and eleven years old. We played cards, draughts and other indoor games but I went there to be enthralled with his enchanting children's tales, elaborate anecdotes, but most of all his eerie, macabre, grisly stories of the nefarious Edinburgh pair, Burke and Hare. He mesmerized me with gruesome, frightening accounts of newly dead bodies being stealthily dug up from the graves in the middle of the night and quickly wheeled away and sold for money.

He could recite lengthy tales of fearsome facts in a deep ghostly voice, keeping me fascinated and spellbound for hours with different stories in the dimly lit room night after night. I remember well his long purposeful pauses, his blue eyes that twinkled with mischief and merriment, enabling fear to strike home before proceeding with the remainder of the tale, while I waited with staring eyes and bated breath for him to continue. Taking in every word I felt the shivers run up and down my spine as his story progressed. Soon it was bedtime and I had to creep out into the dark portentous night to my own home. He knew I was afraid and usually came with me to the door. I would undress for bed all a-tingle and excited. I found it was difficult to get to sleep, but even then I was looking forward to the next evening.

At one stage we had the idea that we were not growing up fast enough. The hairs on our bodies weren't making adequate

progress towards manhood, so we decided to do something
about it. The local pit wagons and railway siding lay alongside
the cottages. After the day's work was done and the shunting,
clinking and clanging had stopped, we jumped the lines to
reach the wagons. From the boxes situated underneath each
wagon we collected handfuls of grease, plastering it all over us
to grow up more quickly. The stealthy exercise went on for
weeks. Each day we would closely inspect each other to
discover what progress was being achieved. Nothing much
materialized but at that time some of the older members of the
gang were indeed growing up, and the younger ones took
encouragement from what they saw. We plastered ourselves
even more. Whether it had any effect, who can tell.

Sunday School attendance was obligatory, but for me it meant a
waste of playing time. The teachings at Sunday School were to
me intrinsically worthless. I paid little attention to the religious
instructions and only went there to sing the hymns and be with
the crowd. I was completely unaware of the denomination. It
could have been any one of the four creeds prevalent in
Scotland – Baptist, Methodist, Presbyterian and Episcopalian
were all the same to me. I knew I was not a hypocritical
church-going Roman Catholic and didn't want to be one. There
was little animosity towards Roman Catholics but there was
some discrimination. We all knew they were different: their
church, funerals, drunken wakes, and other activities were
somewhat mysterious and incomprehensible.

As I grew up I did occasionally attend a church, trying to
find religion, but it was hopeless. To sit there, compelled to
listen to the monotone utterances of the minister, most of which
couldn't be heard because of the church acoustics, caused total
lack of interest. Each time I attended the sermons seemed too

long, and I found myself waiting impatiently for the tedious service to be over. I was dissuaded from further search. No one has been able to convince or convert me to any faith, so consequently I have remained a sceptic and agnostic. At no time have I experienced a serous religious phase. In my heart I have hoped and yearned for religion but it has never come yet. Perhaps it will!

My early days at primary school were happy times. I was always keen to go to lessons and found it great to be back at school after the long summer holidays. Some kids actually hated it. I was seldom absent. Only dire necessity kept me away from class. I hated missing a lesson and getting behind. My virulent attack of scarlet fever caused the only long absence I can remember. I found most subjects easy to assimilate and listened attentively to all that was taught. I was quick at arithmetic, good at geography and engineering drawing, fair at history and art, but even though I had no difficulties in learning to read, my practical use of English and English composition were barely average. I had a limited vocabulary and a lamentable facility for remembering words; consequently I had problems recalling any reading previously undertaken. This affected my English written work which to say the least was prosaic. Having a paucity of originality and with imaginative limitations, I lacked the confidence to invent. When I did have a flash of inspiration I was too self conscious, embarrassed and under-confident to put it down on paper. With this perpetual fear of making mistakes and subsequently suffering the ridicule that followed, as witnessed in other kids who tried, it was sufficient for me to present only mundane material. Even with this weakness in the use of the English language, oral and written, I managed to pass the eleven plus examinations at the age of ten and was awarded a school prize. It was a book, of all things, but I can't recall its name.

By passing my eleven plus examination I was eligible to proceed to the better of the two advanced schools in the area. It taught French and Latin, one of which was compulsory. With my inherent disability in English it was the last place I wanted to go, so I elected for the secondary school with the majority of my classmates. On reflection it was a crucial error, a missed opportunity for better education caused solely by lack of parental attention and guidance. Parents and relatives were not interested in our education. As long as we went to school and didn't play truant they were satisfied and totally oblivious to our educational needs and aspirations. There were no stimulating words of encouragement, no rewards and no one offered advice.

One particularly overt and irritating trait of mine at primary school was my eagerness to show how clever I was, a touch of the unattractive narcissism within some of us. My pretentious habit was to finish the arithmetical problems issued to the class quickly. When I had finished well ahead of the others I used to sit myself up on the rear of my seat. This was done to attract the teacher's attention and he always played my game. He would point his finger at me and shout: 'Kyle, get down off your perch', in a loud voice. He knew why I was sitting there and his recognition was sufficient to satisfy my ego; he never told me to stop it. All the class of course were aware of the incident which was the purpose of the exercise. Some kids got cross; from others there was a ripple of applause. I was always ready to elicit approval from new admirers at this stage.

The English teacher was a frail red-haired woman with a Roman nose. She was a petite, prim and prudish middle-aged spinster, who blushed profusely at the least little upset. She had little control over us and therefore suffered a good deal of naughtiness from the mixed class of boys and girls. Corporal punishment was part of school discipline and the leather strap, peculiar to Scottish schools, was the instrument used to carry out the necessary. When called out for the 'belt', each of us in turn would swagger out, holding out our hands with an arrogant wink at the rest of the class. After receiving six strokes of the best, three on each hand, we went back to our seats smiling. Teacher by this time would be embarrassed and flushed as red as a beetroot, hot and bothered with all her inept exertions. Even the girls who sometimes shed a tear as they returned to their seats enjoyed the pathetic situation she found herself in. The English lessons were of little value because of the teacher's usurped authority.

My four years at secondary public school passed without anything of significance taking place. I continued conscientiously at my lessons; the subjects at which I was good at the primary stage made adequate progress at the higher level. Mathematics was my best accomplishment and chief source of interest. The next step in the curriculum would have been trigonometry and an introduction to differential and integral calculus, but regrettably I was never given the chance.

I never voluntarily did any private study and only completed the minimum amount of homework supplied by the school. Not one of us ever contemplated or was ever encouraged to work at home, so most homework was completed on the way home from school. We would stop in a group, sit on the grass by the roadside, complete the work and arrive home free to indulge in our never-ending play.

The English language was still by far my weakest subject, and even though I passed the final examination it was recommended by the education authorities that I attend English further education classes at Hamilton Academy to attain a more satisfactory standard. This recommendation I adhered to for a year but it made little impact on my fluency, spoken or written. I was still relatively inarticulate. However, I had a retentive facility for numbers and could relate, for example, the results of the forty-six English Football League games any time within the next forty-eight hours. I could also recall lengthy telephone numbers, and other digital problems were easily committed to memory. So despite being singularly incapable of mastering English or indeed any language I had a capacity of reeling off a litany of statistics. This led me to a life of facts and figures, and not phrases. With some temerity I'm now endeavouring to alter the balance.

I gained prominence at school sports, and had a natural aptitude for ball games. I particularly favoured the pentathlon field and track events, and won a small cup for the best all round athlete. My main sport, however, was soccer and that developed so well at a young age that I was selected for a trial game to represent Scotland. The sports master told the team that I was the fastest boy in the school with a ball at my feet. I'm sure that if war had not come along I would almost certainly have become a professional footballer. But I never finished my trial game for Scotland. I was unfortunate enough to be kicked hard on the shins and was forced to leave the field.

The only social event I recall during the years at secondary school was an outing arranged by the school authorities to witness the launching of the liner the *Queen Mary* on the River Clyde. We were taken by the busload for an unusual and exciting day, and watched the great liner make her slow ponderous slide down the slipway, sirens blowing, and gathering speed as she splashed into the water. She wasn't the only thing that got wet. It was pouring with rain.

There were four picture houses which we patronized in our local towns, all scented and sprayed with disinfectant. I loved the pictures. Up to the age of eleven I attended every Saturday afternoon, queueing up for the matinée where some kids, even at a penny fee, tried to squeeze in for nothing.

British Movietone News presenting the truth to the 'three' peoples of the world came first. It was years before I realized that, 'three' was in fact 'free'. There was usually a 'double bill'. There would be a dramatic feature film, and a rendering of some thriller which kept us on the edge of our seats.

Or there could be a current cowboys and Indians film, or a *Tarzan* serial, or both. Serials went on for weeks, chapter after chapter, always ending abruptly at a crucial moment. It was annoying to have to wait until next week to see what happened. Reeling out blinking into the sunlight we would play the part on the way home, with the noisy hollering call of Tarzan or the sound of gunfire being heard for miles around our neighbourhood.

Such are my happy recollections of the innocence and simplicity which marked our way of life as children in one of the most deprived mining communities; they were paralleled all over Scotland. We enjoyed our unrestricted simple pleasures. We made our own entertainment. We lacked proper food and material things, but enjoyed ourselves, completely unaware of the poverty we lived in or the existence of the rest of the world.

We were of unsure arrogance in our own environment. We lived in the old tradition, were self-disciplined in an age when good and evil, right and wrong were sharply defined. None of our vigorous escapades was ever violent, nor did we have any significant trouble with the law. No one took advantage of or harassed the individual, the old or innocent. We took our chances at play with our own legs and limbs, sometimes with our lives it seemed; but we remained contagiously optimistic. No envy or pessimistic thoughts ever spoiled my early adventurous childhood playground.

Now and again I would speculate what the future held for me. I had no idea what work I was likely to do on leaving school. One thing was certain, I wouldn't go down the mines. There was no real promise for the future. I was pitifully ignorant of the outside world and whatever work I undertook would be local. I nursed three extravagant ambitions. To toy with these dreams and egotistical aspirations, which were as accessible as getting to the moon and beyond, seemed ludicrous. I craved for excitement and had a deep desire to fly, to be a pilot. I also wanted very much to travel and discover America, as love of the cinema fired my imagination and enthusiasm for the glamorous far-off fantasy land of Hollywood that existed on the big screen. Finally I wanted to play the blues saxophone.

Those high ambitions were extraordinary in my particular environment, and only with a massive change of circumstances could they materialize. There seemed not the remotest chance of any one of these wild imaginings ever coming true. Strangely enough one evening, while collecting a female friend who was having her horoscope read by a remarkable clairvoyant, I was inveigled into having mine done. That woman told me I would soon leave Scotland and find myself in a far-off land. I would wear a type of uniform, meet and marry a dark haired girl and do much travelling. As I left she said that I too was mediumistic, so I found the reading a bit of a laugh.

Fate was to play its hand sooner than expected. The clairvoyant's words have remained a source of intrigue ever since.

I left school in the summer of 1937 at the age of fourteen, the age accepted then as being old enough to work and wear long trousers. I had attained six higher school leaving certificates, the equivalent of 'O' levels in England.

So in mid-winter 1937 I was dispatched to work in the engineer's dungaree-and-boiler-suit brigade without my consent. That first start in life was manipulated for me. My six 'O' levels had, it seemed, been good enough to take me out of the mining environment. I started work as a plater's apprentice. Work consisted of lifting uncut steel plates and angles on to a bench, and marking them manually using a steel scribe, hammer and punch. Each plate or angle was marked for cutting and drilling as indicated on the blueprints or wooden templates supplied by the drawing office or template workroom. We used woollen mitts in the winter to prevent our hands sticking to the cold steel. For the Motherwell Bridge Engineering Company I worked a forty-four hour week for the grand sum of 9*s* 1½*d*, of which 6*d* was deducted, leaving a pitifully inadequate take home pay of 8*s* 7½*d* – small remuneration for a week of exhausting exertions.

The wage packet was diligently handed over to my guardian, as my mother was now dead. Each week I would be given 6*d* pocket money. It provided me with a packet of five cheap Woodbine cigarettes for 2*d* and left me 4*d* for the front stalls at the local cinema on a Saturday night.

Travelling to work was not easy. For thirty minutes each day, morning and evening, I braved the elements and cycled a round trip of eight miles. This went on for three years. In the bitterly cold inclement weather of the winter, one's hands and feet were frozen on arrival. I usually arrived safe at work without accident or hindrance. One day on my way to work in the early morning, cycling downhill into a blizzard, head tucked down, I crashed full tilt into the side of a bus. It was passing on the main road at ninety degrees to my approach. Visibility was poor; timing was perfect. I lay concussed, bruised and bleeding and was eventually carried away, waking up in a doctor's surgery. I recovered well enough and with only a slight headache and amnesia, was soon declared fit to continue on my way to work. As I cycled along, worried about being late for work, punctuality being a mania, I calculated I had lost two hours' pay, which would make the pay packet even smaller. Financial prudence was strong in all of us, and financial independence the material goal in life. There would be repercussions, I imagined. Money was hard to come by and all of us knew its value only too well. I even wondered if I would get my pocket money at the end of that week – but I did.

During the apprenticeship, which thankfully lasted only three years, I had many problems with some of the obnoxious individuals among whom I worked. Their pranks, abuse of authority and ambivalent attitudes towards the young caused much frustration and unhappiness among us. As apprentices we were continually intimidated. There were many altercations. I refused to be provoked but one day, baited beyond endurance, I couldn't control myself. An unbearable discontent seized possession of me. Every fibre of my body was retaliating and with my instinctive pugnacity I let fly. Several times before I had felt antagonistic, but had managed to contain my feelings until then. The bellicose, incompatible character who was supposed to be training me was on the receiving end. We fought and fell over rows of angles and steel plates, stood up and fell again, until the fight was stopped.

He was ostracized by other enraged apprentices. We manifested our displeasure and took revenge by being maliciously obstructive, uncooperative and unhelpful when most needed. He was moved to another department, and I made significant and rapid progress with my job. Being diligent and conscientious my work pleased my employers, and soon I was working on my own, given my own bench and earning an extra 2s per week. I would probably have been content to qualify at that type of work after a five year apprenticeship, but even then I had my eye on better things. I had already requested an interview for the higher academic skills of the drawing office. I wanted to be a draughtsman if only to get away from this manual toil. At that time all my aspirations stopped there. I didn't succeed then, but I managed to accomplish it some ten years later with a small light engineering firm in Stroud, Gloucestershire, after the war.

When I was sixteen I decided to take up ballroom dancing. I attended the Masonic Town Hall dances held once a week on a Saturday evening instead of making my usual jaunt to the cinema.

I was sixteen but emotionally years younger. Being basically shy and apprehensive it was difficult initially finding a partner. I plucked up enough courage to approach the girls who were left on the floor on the other side of the hall, after the better looking ones were on the dance floor. They may not have been the prettiest, but they were often the better dancers. With their help I made good progress moving in easy rhythm and became competent at the waltz, the slow and quick foxtrots and the quickstep. The more intricate steps of the tango took longer to master and as the music stopped sometimes we were left in suspended animation in a comical position, so I avoided it for a while. I enjoyed the others very much.

I danced to tunes like 'Blue Moon', 'Blueberry Hill', 'Red Sails in the Sunset', 'Jealousy', 'In the Mood' and many more. The smooth ballroom dancing style renowned of the Scots and Scotland, which I acquired in a short space of time in that small inconsequential hall, paid large dividends and brought forth many delightful partners during my extensive travels.

Now that I had got used to girls, I tried to obtain more female company, and joined the boys on their Sunday night vigil. In our best Sunday clothes and shoes, our hair Brylcreemed, we would stroll the main thoroughfare between the two towns of Motherwell and Hamilton looking for girls to date. That broad straight road, stretching two miles, and crossing over the River Clyde was packed with groups of both sexes, all out on a fraternization trip. I had a discerning eye for a pretty face. Most of the time it was just that, looking, talking, saying 'Hello' in passing but never touching. They remained elusive and were strange but by now desirable creatures well out of my reach.

It was then 1939 and to date I had led a humdrum sheltered existence acquiring only the bare necessities of life. Repression of emotions and expression were part of a way of life for the working class in Scotland. Overall I was completely impervious to these austere conditions that had been mine, never having mixed with anything better. I was seventeen, five feet seven inches tall, with dark hair with a suggestion of a wave, blue eyes and slightly dimpled chin. I had no pimples and didn't go through the acne-susceptible teenage stage; nor did the anticipated deficiency diseases due to earlier dietary inadequacies happen. All in all, I was considered to be a good looking young boy! Socially, though, I was introverted and inhibited by a deathly shyness, not yet confident in strange company.

Then the momentous event that sliced across the dullness of my existence took place, and a hopeful flash of light unexpectedly streaked through. Soon those spartan years of childhood and adolescence were to end and fortunes were to change dramatically. Within a year I was to leave this bleak purgatory, never to return. This life of economic stress and poverty was over. It was a brave new world that I entered, a world with a rate of change for which I was socially and mentally unprepared. The quality of life suddenly changed key.

Adolf Hitler at Berchtesgaden at the
beginning of the war

The advent of Hitler's new order, the Third Reich, and the
phenomenal rise of National Socialism in Nazi Germany,
culminating in the blitzkreig invasion of Poland and the
democratic answer of the Allies to destroy it, ordained my
future and extraordinary good fortune. Mr Chamberlain's piece
of white paper blowing in the wind with his message of peace
in our time thankfully meant his time and not mine.

The will of fate and the war were the causes of my liberation
and fulfilment of my life's main ambition. What at one time
seemed infinitely remote became a possibility and finally a
reality. Being born and bred in a mining community
environment where living was rough and tough, the spirit was
tenaciously aggressive and the temper quick to retaliate if
provoked.

When the Second World War began I was just that little too
young to participate. I was also serving an apprenticeship in
engineering, a reserved occupation. However, I joined the local

Air Training Corps to gain as much general service knowledge as possible, to enhance my prospects when I came of age. I attended evening classes at the local High School twice a week where elementary lessons on all aspects of service life were offered. I studied aircraft silhouette identification, getting to know many British and German current aircraft types, and was given an introduction to morse code. After some weeks' practice I was able to send eight words and receive four, it being easier to send than to receive. That practical application was to prove beneficial when sitting my pilot's wings examination some months later, for one needed to send twelve and receive eight words to pass. It was easy to step up to that amount.

Other subjects pertinent to the Air Force, like service ranks, basic meteorology and simple navigation were covered, and were most helpful at a later stage. Thus I spent my life in limbo anxiously waiting to grow old enough to join the war, while the Battle of Britain was in full flight.

CHAPTER 2

A Wish and a Star

I volunteered to fly for the Royal Air Force in early February 1941 and was called for my first interview and reception at Kelvin Hall, Glasgow some six weeks later.

Probably I was being inordinately ambitious for my lowly status, but I had plenty of energy and self-confidence. I *knew* I could fly, given the chance. I was continually criticized by my workmates, young and old, for being over ambitious, unlikely to succeed, without the academic qualifications; nor did I know anything about aerodynamics. As I left for the interview they were sceptical, and thought my chances of acceptance were nil.

There were a large number of young hopefuls from all over Scotland on that particular spring day, all eager, but there were to be many, many disappointments even at that early stage. From information announced at the end of the day, only seventy-seven were accepted from the hundreds interviewed to go forward to the next stage, to be held in Edinburgh. It promised well that I'd passed. Anxiously I awaited the post daily, but another six weeks elapsed – during which time my mind wasn't on my work – before I was told to proceed for further interview and selection at the Scottish capital. It was with great trepidation that I travelled that particular journey.

I took part in comprehensive intelligence and aptitude examinations and stripped naked for a harsh medical test, from which there were again many failures. With all preliminary tests completed, there began the interminable impatient wait for the results. It was a nerve-racking, nail-biting experience, not knowing whether or not one would progress to the interview.

I was ushered in to confront the board in due course. There were many questions to answer. Sometimes I felt it was simply an investigative personal cross-examination and I found that particularly taxing. There were lengthy questions on current affairs, recently given attention for the first time in my life. Questions on sport, hobbies, mental arithmetic problems and other general topics came from each board member in turn. Having spent a year in the Air Training Cadets was most helpful with the military matters.

'What would you do if you found a nest of wasps?'

'Destroy them,' I answered in a flash.

'Good,' they said.

'What papers do you read?'

'The *Daily Mail*,' I answered.

'Why?' they said.

'Because I like to read it,' I replied.

They looked at one another and nodded.

It seems some people when asked this question had replied, the *Daily Telegraph*. They were then asked who the air correspondent was and what he had written yesterday. Of course they couldn't answer, as they didn't read the *Telegraph*. With a sudden stab of perception I stuck to the truth. It was this they approved of. I was not naturally gifted in written or oral communication, but my truthfulness and alertness of mind in answering all their searching questions, particularly in mental arithmetic, helped me pass the interview.

After what seemed a lengthy period of deliberation and consultation, I remember being clearly informed by one fatuous older member of the board, I guessed he must have been forty, that even though I was being accepted for pilot training, I would never make a navigator! I failed to comprehend his remark at the time, but smiling I bent my head in acquiescence. Anyway, who wanted to be a navigator, I thought; I wanted to be a fighter pilot, so I couldn't have cared

Somewhere in Scotland, 1941, having volunteered for aircrew

less. Also I wasn't really listening; all I could hear was that I had passed. I think in hindsight that he was inferring I wasn't academically good enough to qualify as a navigator. I didn't have the prerequisite 'A' levels nor the maturity to be trained for them. As a matter of interest I was to prove him wrong by coming top of a specialist pilot navigator course, albeit some twenty years later.

The intrinsically important point then was that I had passed the main selection board, one of only seven selected, and had been recommended for pilot training. That first crucial hurdle over, I was indeed exultant as I quietly closed the door behind me on leaving the interview room. The euphoric glow and high expectations, however, didn't blind me to the fact that further strenuous academic and aptitude tests lay ahead. Everything was going to be a monumental challenge.

With time to spare before catching the train home, I walked jauntily on air, along popular picturesque Princes Street. It was a joy to linger gazing at the goodies on display in the shop windows, feeling just a little envious. On that cold clear day, on impulse and with a tingle of pleasure, I continued towards Edinburgh castle, climbing the escarpment to a high viewpoint that gave me a wonderful panoramic picture of the city and the Firth of Forth. Literally and metaphorically, the climb to greater heights and wider horizons was imminent.

The train journey home was quiet. I had much to think about while waiting for call up. It was with a deep and joyful satisfaction that I broke the news to all concerned.

The OHMS (On His Majesty's Service) letter duly arrived, stating that I had to report to Lord's Cricket Ground, St John's Wood, London on the palindromic date of 14.7.41. I read the letter starry eyed, thrilled and excessively excited, but soon after felt quite apprehensive. I had never travelled further than a few miles from home before, except for a visit to Edinburgh, and now I was going all the way to England. The thought of travelling to London was daunting in itself, but the shortage of cash and clothes was also a problem. I had little of either.

I had nothing to pack except a towel, a shirt, a pair of recently acquired pyjamas and some toilet gear. With my last week's wages I purchased a cheap pair of dark brown suede shoes, leaving almost no money to travel with. With this extraordinary light baggage and pathological desire to get away from my background, I caught the overnight train south. No one saw me to the station, and there was no sentimental parting – only an anxious concern on my part as I boarded the train for what I considered a complicated journey to a destination I'd never heard of, a place infinitely remote and mysterious called Lord's Cricket Ground, London. It could have been Baghdad or Timbuktu.

The journey by train down to London was quiet. I was restless as I watched the dreary industrial outlook of the town I had lived in all my life fade away. It felt strange to be on an overnight train to England, leaving home for good. The first part of the journey was uneventful and I dozed through the hours of darkness until we stopped at Carlisle, and again until we reached Crewe. When dawn came I was awake and inquisitive, peering through the misty windows at the racing countryside covered in white smoke streaming back from the engine, waiting with a touch of trepidation, until the arrival of the train at Euston station in the early morning. Odd snatches of conversation of no particular interest took place with passengers in transit.

I left the train and walked tentatively towards the station exit. The next problem was to find my way across London, this great cosmopolitan city, but how? The hugeness of the city was appalling as I stepped from Euston station into the street and mingled with the early morning crowds. With no guide I was utterly lost among eight million strangers. London, I realized soon, was alien, large and impersonal with streams of anonymous people passing by. It remains so today.

I had two options of travel, either to go by underground or take the bus. The tube seemed too complex, so I chose what was in fact the most difficult mode of travel and crossed London by various buses. With each change of bus en route any uncertainties of direction were resolved by enquiring about the correct bus number to the next stage. Not everyone was able to help. After a while I arrived at my destination, scarcely able to believe I'd made it, but with much satisfaction that I had arrived all by myself.

They came trickling in all day, the long, the short and the tall. By evening they were arriving in prodigious numbers, hundreds of young men who were processed for attestation and integrated into flights of fifty. There was much speculation and continual chattering. We were allocated bunk beds, and informed to get a good night's sleep, as we would be awake at the crack of dawn. There was little time to get to know anyone. Conversation was of necessity limited before lights out.

I lay there in my bunk that night absolutely mesmerized with all the edifying activities of the day – liberated from old restrictions and trying to sort out my reactions to my first day in England in the Royal Air Force, wondering how the future would unfold. They were an extremely mixed bunch around me. As I drifted off to sleep I wondered if I would be able to compete with these confident, well-spoken, well-educated and to me 'posh' and privileged alien contemporaries.

I kept a passive front for a few days, but the transition was easy with the help of a friend and I managed satisfactorily. The two weeks passed noisily in these tightly packed billets with limited washing facilities. We took it in turns to use these facilities one section at a time.

In our newly issued blue uniforms, the proper size with only small tailored adjustments, we were instructed in the technique of marching, drilling and saluting. There were constant parades for all meals from dawn to dusk, with kit inspections and extra square-bashing in between.

There was practice in the use of gas masks, gas drill coming daily during the first morning parade. Respirators were torn from the satchel and donned as quickly as possible, the corporal's aggressive commands assuring him of our undivided attention. We were certainly proficient soon enough. The holdall strap had to be repositioned between the first two highly burnished buttons of the uniform as we marched off or else we were at the mercy and sadistic whim of the corporal.

There were many inspections of bunks, clothing and accommodation. Some people complained, but this inauguration into the highly disciplined service life did not hold any qualms for me. I had no complaints, except that I didn't like the bacon and baked beans and coffee tainted with bromide for breakfast. I had never tasted any such luxuries before. Others around the table ate voraciously, and nothing was left for the dustbin.

I was number 1345427 aircraftsman Kyle on the grand sum of 2s 6d per day, 17s 6d per week, all of it my own. That was more than double my pay for a forty-four hour week as an apprentice engineer. The fundamental injustice of economic hardship and my previous way of existence had been forever resolved. At last I had achieved financial independence. It was a recurring thought.

After a two week reception period I was posted from the surrounds of St John's Wood to No. 1 Initial Training Wing at Babbacombe, two miles east of Torquay, in Devon. The newly opened training wing was having its administrative teething troubles with some lectures and sporting activities adversely affected by inept timing, inadequate facilities and bad programming. We were the second course sent there and, with many other personnel pouring in with indecent haste shortly afterwards, the staff and facilities were completely overloaded for a time. However, by the end of our six week stay the unit was transformed, and had become efficient and highly organized.

There were a great many parades, followed by intensive periods of drill and excessive amounts of physical training and organized games. In addition to all this exercise, I spent many hours with the Welsh physical training instructor, a Flight Sergeant Lewis, knocking a football about on the Downs high above Oddicombe beach. He had been a professional footballer before call up and represented his country. He reminded me of Stanley Matthews in looks and ball control.

I found exercise no problem, and the life was tough and exhilarating. I was fully fit from my Scottish playground and my year spent with the Air Cadets. I did not drink and drugs were unheard of. So it was inexplicable when, one early morning on parade, I collapsed with dizziness. There was no discernible cause for fainting. I was never so physically and mentally tough in my life, and nobody diagnosed the cause. Under much more stressful conditions it never happened again, and so remains a mystery.

We were billeted in a large white hotel overlooking the bay. The food was good and accommodation excellent; the weather was fine, warm and sunny and I was content in this pleasant active environment. I had never had it so good. I began the basic studies in all the subjects required for pilots. The new curriculum was comprehensive and full of new and interesting subjects. Mastering them required a prodigious effort. I gave them undivided attention because this course was of paramount importance. My single mindedness was such that when others were playing I was accelerating my studies and burning midnight oil, most unusual for me, but I was determined to pass.

The lessons connected with flying, such as principles of flight, flying and airmanship, navigation, meteorology, maps and charts, radio, instruments and engines I found fascinating. Other general lectures on service knowledge, administration, Air Force law and air operations were also unusually interesting. There was nothing academically difficult to understand in any of those lessons but the amount of detail to be remembered in a short space of time seemed massive. To remember for exams details on lift, drag, variation, deviation, the formation of high and low pressure systems with their associated clouds, fronts, fogs, the construction and use of maps and charts, explanation of radio frequencies and wavelengths, types of gyros, air and vertical speed indicators, basic engine knowledge and servicing, together with general service know-how about discipline, morale, survival, intelligence and security was a formidable task.

I used a particular technique to develop and aid my memory to cope with this vast amount of detail. The idea was to build a word, a word easy to remember, from the lengthy answers to individual questions. It was then a simple task to expand and unravel that word in detail to answer the question in full, should it arise in subsequent examinations. A simple example is the word 'RIDE', used to remember the means of imparting information. No matter how ambiguous or rhetorical the subject was, finding a word to simplify it was a great asset. In this case the answer to the word was *R*epetition, *I*mitation, *D*emonstration, *E*xplanation (RIDE). This simple technique was used and expanded to incorporate many intricate and difficult subjects I had to deal with later. It was an answer to passing exams in general. Everything was reduced to a state of reasonable simplicity. That has always been my aim, in all aspects of life.

With this method the new curriculum taught at Initial Training Wing was easier to assimilate, and progress was more than adequate. I did well in all the exams except for a practical navigation paper in the finals at the end of the course. I was nervous and conscious of possible failure, with its severe consequences, and in my sub-conscious I believe I was psychologically disturbed by that remark made to me about navigation at my Edinburgh selection board. I made a bad error of plotting a magnetic course on the air plot instead of a true course, causing a considerable difference in the size of the 'cocked hat', a triangle formed by three crossed lines. It made the final position of the latitude and longitude co-ordinates some miles in error. I only realized this when discussing the exam with other students afterwards.

We were sent on leave immediately after the examinations at the end of the course, before our next posting, if there was to be one. It was a worrying time and I feared for the future. On return the results were published. I had passed well, except for that navigation paper, which I scraped through by a few marks. My relief was terrific.

The Royal Air Force was teaching me a great deal and I was learning much from the chaps among whom I was living. At this time, however, my spoken English with its Scottish colloquialisms, thick of accent, left a lot to be desired – so much so, that a number of the students couldn't understand me. I decided I'd better do something about it before I began my flying training.

At attestation in London, I had befriended a tall fair-haired, altruistic young Englishman, from Guildford in Surrey. Len Richardson spontaneously offered me guidance and protection until I could stand on my own two feet. He smoked a pipe, which didn't suit him as he looked much too young. We must have had some unknown emotional chemistry pulling us together, as we were to remain loyal pals for the next four years. Only for a period of six months were we apart: he went for his flying training in California and I went to Texas. He had immense vitality, was full of avuncular advice and a paragon of discretion through the years. Len was just the sort of person my tactless, aggressive, inexperienced self needed.

He was the translater of my thick unpleasant Glaswegian accent, my English teacher and my aesthetic mentor in those early days. Our lives were interwoven from the first day we met. On our return from America we were soon together again, meeting on the ship coming home to the UK, going through the British Flying Training Refresher schools, Operational Training unit. Then, happily, we were posted to the same Typhoon squadron.

Our ranks remained equivalent throughout the war, promotion coming along simultaneously. Our squadron responsibilities were similar; our flying awards and commissioning also happened together and we both managed to survive the war. An extraordinary fate had brought about this friendship. He was a natural fighter pilot, with more than his fair share of aptitude and reflex action, and he flew with verve. We flew much together. I remember flying from Tangmere to our forward base, happily touching wingtips, just for the hell of it. It is sad to relate that Len Richardson was killed when leading his flight of four Tempest aircraft down through low cloud into the Hampshire hills in 1947. Until then he had been my closest friend.

CHAPTER 3

To the Land of Plenty

By October 1941 I was bound for America to begin flying training. Hundreds of potential pilots were assembled at an RAF Holding Unit in the Midlands, awaiting transport across the Atlantic Ocean.

I remained at RAF Wilmslow for a month before boarding a train for the point of departure at Greenock, Scotland, where the French liner *Louis Pasteur* was berthed awaiting shipment of servicemen and civilian passengers who were travelling to the United States and Canada. One Battle of Britain pilot I had heard about, called Stanford-Tuck, made himself known to all the potential pilots when we were assembled for a short question and answer session in the ship's cinema. I kept thinking he seemed much older than me. He was little seen during the voyage, as he was travelling the equivalent of first class and we were all in the hold. Some budding pilots wanted to meet him personally. I admired and envied his wings and gongs, but I was never to be a hero worshipper.

The indefinite wait aboard ship at Greenock Docks on the Clyde, with a full and overcrowded complement of men while the large convoy assembled nearby, had been frustrating. Exploration of the large liner was interesting but all aboard were restless as the delay continued.

Then one night in late October, quite unexpectedly, she sailed. Goodbye Britain for a while, we thought. Great expectations lay ahead. Excitement flared as the ship's shops were thrown wide open that first night as we slowly sailed down the Clyde to rendezvous with the convoy. Nearly everyone injudiciously stuffed themselves full with copious

Just before I was posted to
America, October 1941. The
white flash on the cap indicates
aircrew training

amounts of the goodies available. It tasted like manna; we
hadn't seen such varieties of luscious food, fruit and
sweetstuffs for a considerable time. Euphoria was high as the
night progressed and it was late evening before we tumbled our
way towards our tightly packed hammocks, somewhere down
in the bowels of the ship.

We were all soon to rue our rapacious activities of the night.
Before dawn the next morning the convoy had sailed into the
teeth of a gigantic howling storm off the northern coast of
Ireland. Waves of titanic proportions tossed us about like a leaf
in a torrent.

I awoke to a commotion of moans and groans throughout the
bulkhead. In the darkness I couldn't fathom what was wrong,
but the cause was obvious. Seconds after awakening I began to
feel queer, cold with vertigo, then violently ill. Struggling from
the hammock I made my way swiftly to the uppermost deck of
the ship, gasping for cool fresh air. On arrival I found the deck

was littered with bodies in various stages of undress, sprawled in extraordinary positions everywhere. I joined the bedraggled sick crowd and remained on the upper deck walking back and forth, gulping great intakes of cold fresh air for the next twenty-four hours. No one attempted to go inside into the warmth of the ship, for obvious reasons. The white-topped mountainous seas continued. In due course we all recovered as we rode out the brutal storm and were able to creep back to our cramped, claustrophobic to some, but warm overcrowded hammocks. We occasionally struggled to get into them but nobody fell out during the voyage. These living conditions were readily accepted by everyone and a friendly atmosphere and a sense of adventure permeated through the rest of our eventful journey.

The battle for the Atlantic was nearing its zenith late in 1941. Had the German submarines attacked our convoy on that first day at sea, they would surely have had us all at their mercy. We were all sea-sick, I for one couldn't have cared less, but fortunately they didn't strike till later. The U-boats made their presence felt after some two days at sea and as I was fully recovered I was able to enjoy the excitement of emergency lifeboat drills and the general commotion of action. We watched the destroyers and other escort vessels chasing the submarines around the ocean, hooting, signalling, manoeuvring and steaming after them towards the horizon. This first attack was warded off without casualties and it was a thrilling experience to be involved in action.

Twice more the convoy was attacked before reaching the safety of American waters; the main attack was made in the area known as the Black Gap in mid-Atlantic. That was an area of a few hundred miles in the middle of 3,000 miles of ocean, where most of the convoy's escort ships were unable to maintain full cover because of their limited range. This left the convoys completely unprotected. Naturally the enemy was aware of our inadequate cover, hence the numerous victorious attacks made by them in the Black Gap.

Our convoy of thirty ships had the speed of advance of the slowest ship, about 10 to 12 knots, and didn't escape the U-boats' attention. During that scrimmage there were a number of hits on a transport ship and a destroyer; one enemy submarine was reported to have been sunk. There were further alarms, mostly during the night, when precautionary warnings were broadcast to all aboard. We carried out standard life-belt drill, rushing to boat stations, but no more attacks materialized.

Soon afterwards the convoy was considered to be in safe water and the *Louis Pasteur* was given permission to forge ahead on her own. She picked up speed quickly and immediately left the convoy trailing behind, gradually increasing speed to a maximum 28 knots on a fast course for Canada. Within two more days the liner docked at Halifax, in Nova Scotia, Canada and with great haste we were all disembarked. Tremulous with expectations, I remember stepping on to foreign soil realizing that I had arrived on the New Continent. I was to have six glorious months ahead of me.

I remained in Canada for a week at a newly constructed but wet and cold camp called Moncton, in New Brunswick. It was so muddy that everyone was issued with Wellington boots to move around. Squelching through the stuff daily up to our knees at times became an intolerable burden for us all; we couldn't move more than a few yards from the billets to the large cafeteria-style messing hall and back. After being stuck for a week in the mire we were happy when news came through of our next move; would we hand in our Wellington boots?

We were sorted into batches of fifty. I rushed forward from the crowd with indecent haste to be in the first batch and was the last man allowed in. My friend Len Richardson was one behind me when the cut was made and he was stopped from joining me. So I was sent to Terrell, Texas and he was dispatched to Glendale, California, with the second fifty. I could have kicked myself, irate at losing my friend and envious of his posting, as I had much wanted to see Hollywood. Others went to Mesa in Arizona and to three other British Flying Training Schools throughout the United States (Clewiston in Florida, and Miami and Ponca City in Oklahoma). Some also went to Pensacola in Florida to be trained under the jurisdiction of the United States Navy, where strong rumour had it that the 'scrub rate' was fantastic.

So we boarded our specially prepared Pullman trains, taking us to our very different destinations. I took the long, slow four day journey to Texas, the Lone Star State in the deep south of the land of the free. The journey took us through miles and miles of vast stretches of barren country, where nothing penetrated the horizon. We passed famous towns and cities like Montreal, Toronto, Chicago, St Louis and finally came to Dallas. I gazed with rapture at the many sights en route, particularly noticing the central core of skyscrapers in every city as we pulled into and out of the stations.

On our journey south I first tasted southern fried chicken and also for the first time set eyes on the now ubiquitous black man, many of whom served us on the long tiresome trek to the giant state of Texas. We slept in our seats. The days were spent reading and writing, playing friendly games of cards, chess, draughts or singing the latest hits, or songs of the First World War. 'It's a long way to Tipperary, it's a long way to go' seemed appropriate. Then we discussed and speculated what lay ahead: how many of us would succeed and how many were likely to fail; and how glad we were not to be going to Pensacola. What would the camp be like? And the girls?

The long journey continued. The train plunged on through the darkness and we slept. We arrived in Dallas on 2 November 1941. Those four days on the train had left an indelible mark on my memory and will always remain. I promised myself that one day I would return to explore the grandeur of this country, as I had begun to comprehend the vastness of America.

I joined No. 1 British Flying Training School, the first British Flying Training School (BFTS) to commence functioning in America. Flying had started at Love Field, Dallas in June 1941, but soon it moved thirty miles east to the small township of Terrell, where it remained until it was disbanded towards the end of the war. Little did I realize then that I would be driving past that small airfield some forty years later, wallowing in a nostalgic journey, driving from New Orleans via Dallas to Denver; I was helping my eldest son move house by driving a rental truck across Louisiana, Texas and Colorado.

The six BFTSs established throughout the United States before Pearl Harbor were highly regarded and highly successful. They had been organized to increase the flow of pilots urgently needed after the Battle of Britain and for the eventual invasion of Europe. Like every new venture the BFTSs had their growing pains. Difficulties in supplies and equipment, adjusting to American-type flying training and American instructors, and also to some extent the language, caused problems. However, all were overcome and the BFTS qualified to take their place among the other alma maters of the Royal Air Force, training units.

The layout of the camp was impressive, with clean and excellent training facilities and personnel accommodation. The young Americans, men and women, black and white, employed to supply our every need were indeed most courteous,

Part layout of No. 1 BFTS Terrell, Texas, with some of the 'locals'

inquisitive and helpful. All personnel on the staff were affable and unpretentious including our flying instructors, who treated us with the utmost consideration at all times. The school was administered by an RAF Wing Commander and his adjutant flight lieutenant, together with a flight sergeant responsible for discipline. The whole unit was efficiently organized. We as students were privileged and delighted to be part of the whole enterprise.

I walked for the first time with other young hopefuls into the spacious and spotlessly clean dining room for breakfast. The 'juke-box' was loudly rendering 'Brahms Lullaby' and the sweet smell of luscious hot cooking in a warm colourful and cosy atmosphere made it all very inviting. It was like a welcoming to Shangri-La.

While we were having a large breakfast the records changed, and the new tune of the decade was heard throbbing noisily every now and again. The 'Chattanooga Choo Choo' was begging its pardon. Other tunes heard and enjoyed over breakfast that first morning and many more times thereafter, were obviously favourites of the local talent, who sang happily as they served. We had 'The Eyes of Texas', 'The Star Spangled Banner', 'Don't Fence Me In', Tchaikovsky's piano concerto and the appropriate Army Air Corps chorus, 'Off we go into the Wild Blue Yonder', that ended with 'nothing can stop the Army Air Corps'. Except the weather, we quickly added.

After some administrative formalities had been completed we were allowed out of camp that second morning in Texas. All of us were dressed in grey flannel suits provided by our government. America was not yet in the war, the Japanese had not yet attacked Pearl Harbor and uniforms were forbidden.

Avidly awaiting our first glimpse of the local terrain and talent, three of us headed for the camp main exit. On arrival at the gate we were confronted with an enormous number of large automobiles stretching hundreds of yards alongside the airfield's western boundary. They were full of beautiful and some not so beautiful girls and their families awaiting our exit, mainly in fact for members of the now well-established senior course. Others were waiting and willing to express their generosity and southern hospitality towards the newly arrived contingent of young Englishmen.

The three of us passed out the main gate and continued walking towards town. We had gone but a few yards when a large black Buick pulled alongside and the three girls, all seated in the front, shouted out in nasal unison. 'Would you all like a lift into town, boys?' Naturally we were delighted and accepted.

We were soon travelling along the wide highway first having naughtily called at a bootleggers for some cheap bourbon. Texas was a dry state; the rigours of prohibition seemed to have come to stay. The weather was glorious, the car and the country expansive. The attractiveness of it all was tremendous. What a way of life, I thought; may it never end. I was lost in a flood of sensations.

Driving a big black Buick for the first time on the highway near Dallas

One of the girls asked if I would like to drive. I had never sat in the driving seat of any vehicle in my life, but I found myself driving that big black Buick along the broad highway at a speed not quite within the law. Only when requested to turn around did I give in. The car got stuck on the grass verge and I had to move over.

We drove many miles that day, covering large areas of Texas countryside, with its cottonwood trees and drifting tumbling tumbleweed, noisily enjoying ourselves as the illicit whisky began to take its first ever effects. Sex was rearing its ugly head, but not the slightest signs were ever made evident that first day out in Texas. Good sense and shyness forbade anything suggestive.

The billets that evening were alive with stories of our first taste of American hospitality, everyone excitedly relating how they had spent their day. Tomorrow flying would begin and it would be another week before we could meet our American

Stearman PT 18: primary trainer

friends again. The land of life, liberty and the pursuit of happiness had certainly lived up to its glamorous image. We were all most impressed.

Our course was split into two flights, alternating morning and afternoons between flying instruction and ground school and we were given individual instructors.

On 4 November 1941 I started flying as an embryo pilot along with three other students on a Stearman PT 18, a biplane with an open cockpit and a 220 hp engine. I was allocated to an American instructor by the name of J.E. Castleman, a suave, handsome, drawling Texan, whose strong sunburned hand welcomed me to Texas. I grew to like him very much. He was a first class (A1) instructor, and his congenial attitude and charisma infused confidence and experience. Little did I realize then that I would be enacting a similar role, also with four students, ten years later.

During several early trips under his able instruction, I was asked to make a balanced and coordinated stick and rudder level turn, but I used excessive rudder particularly to the left, and skidded the aircraft around. The skid showed on the cockpit instruments, and his drawling Texas accent would come through on the intercom with his popular and fondly remembered expression: 'Kyle, you're riding the piss out of that rudder.'

On my first trip I climbed into the front open cockpit and watched him start the engine, and the propellor sprang into noisy life. That was on an air experience familiarization trip which lasted all of thirty-four minutes according to my log book. As he took off and climbed, I leaned over the side of the cockpit and felt a chill 80 mph wind whipping my face. I lifted my face to the sun, then looked down and around at the wide green expanse of the countryside below. Castleman then made some gentle turns, left and right in the broad blue sky, pointing out some landmarks, but soon we were turning and dipping back towards the airfield. I had barely touched the controls, but exhilaration was bubbling within.

My second trip was intense dual instruction with much to remember. I handled the controls in the air for the first time, initially lightly touching them, then gripping too tightly until my instructor advised me to relax. We went through the functions of each control – stick forward, nose down; stick back, nose up. Each time he would point out the nose in relation to the horizon. Stick to the right, stick to the left, rolling the aircraft, tilting and wings dipping. Those first moments of taut concentration soon passed and I began to get the delicate feel and coordination of the controls.

Ab initio flying consisted at first of take-offs and landings in conjunction with smooth engine handling. We progressed to straight and level flight, shallow and medium turns and gentle climbing turns and descents, aiming to use the aircraft's controls in a smooth coordinated manner before the solo stage. The instructor demonstrated the aircraft's characteristics at the point of incipient stall and spins. He also demonstrated the procedure for a practice forced landing, though not actually landing. These exercises were mandatory in case the necessity arose on first solo. The instructor might initiate you to the more advanced manoeuvres by demonstrating a slow roll or a loop but generally all flying was gentle, and for the student with a good instructor very interesting.

A few more trips of concentrated dual instruction covered all the elementary exercises and I was ready to go solo. We taxied back to dispersal and came to a halt. Castleman left the cockpit with the engine still running, came back and shouted at me over the noise:

'You're OK Kyle; how would you like to go on your own?'

It was unexpected, but how could I refuse?

'Yes please,' I replied.

He gave me a few words of encouragement and left with his parachute for dispersal.

I turned the aircraft and taxied out slowly for take off, tremendously excited and feeling great. Lining up accurately on the runway, I opened the throttle evenly and eased the Stearman into the air. Climbing straight ahead to 500 ft, and checking the airspeed, I turned left, climbing to 1,000 ft. Then I turned downwind, noting myself parallel with the runway. One student at this point got lost and kept straight on, landing at another airfield some 30 miles away. Soon I was turning the aircraft on to base leg, continuing the turn on to the approach path, lining up and rounding out for landing. I was never worried and settled the aircraft for a smooth three point landing. Normally a first landing is a good one for everybody; not so some later attempts!

Going round for the second circuit I had more time to think. Looking down on the airfield I realized it was truly a red letter day for me. To be in sole possession of an aircraft, in Dallas, Texas in such a short space of time gave me a wonderful thrill

First solo flight, Armistice Day, 11 November 1941

of achievement. The difference in my life from six months before was staggering.

I taxied in after landing, manifestly confident and exultant. The thrill of flying enchanted me. My aptitude had been so marked I went solo within a week. It was on Armistice Day, 11 November 1941, about a month before the Japanese attacked Pearl Harbor, and I had only been flying for five hours. In my log book I made a concise remark: '1st Solo, Magic'. I had found my niche.

I recall here a story about another student on an earlier course at a BFTS being asked by his instructor at an early stage in training, if he he would like to attempt a slow roll of the aircraft. On hearing his remark on the student reacted immediately, quickly put the aircraft on its back into a beautiful roll, whereupon the instructor fell out. The student had flown previously of which the instructor was unaware; and being unprepared he was not strapped in. Fortunately his parachute was on and he landed safely.

A celebration was held by the students when the incident became known. During the party a student was thrown into a swimming pool, amid great hilarity. Unfortunately this student couldn't swim and as no one heeded his cries for help as he slowly went down for the third time, he drowned. A verdict of death by misadventure was recorded.

The proportion of flights of dual instruction and solo consolidation changed as we progressed, I was then having two or three solo flights to every dual. Most flights were satisfactory and I enjoyed them immensely, but at times I had a tendency to oscillate between nervousness and arrogant over-confidence, depending on my confidence in the practical air exercise I was performing.

Some flights I flew with complete abandon, soaring and diving with the freedom of an American eagle, each effort reaching a kind of inspired ecstasy. On other flights I overplayed my hand and frightened the daylights out of myself. The more experience I gained, the less the fluctuation, and the frenetic flying soon settled down to a fairly polished display of sequences of aerobatics consistent with my experience.

The weather in Texas was invariably good and I revelled in the clear skies and strong sunlight. With its extremely large fields and non-existent hedgerows the land was a pilot's dream and gave sheer pleasure in an open cockpit. I loved the thrill of flying and the delight of low flying, twisting and turning over and around isolated buildings, tree tops and the scattered low cumulus clouds. I never had any troubles with pure flying. Progress was rapid after first solo. They said that I had a natural propensity for flying and should have no problem in passing the course. These were great words of encouragement and I flew with ever increasing confidence.

Navigational cross-country flights then entered the training syllabus. From these journeys throughout my training I became knowledgeable about the vast state of Texas. Names like Waco,

Witchita Falls, Sherman, Sulphur Springs, Texarkana, Tyler, Ranger, Austin, Amarillo and El Paso were soon familiar.

Due to slight illness at the time of the first solo navigational exercise, I couldn't take part. I was confined to barracks with a touch of flu. Two weeks later I was allowed to do my first solo cross-country and given an individual navigation and meteorological briefing. It was just before Christmas and oddly enough there was a full carpet of snow covering Texas, the first time for eleven years. Everyone was out with their cameras thrilled with the sight of a white Texas.

However, the weather didn't suit a navigational flight much. It wasn't cancelled as it should have been, and I had real difficulties. I set off, a solo aircraft, heading west to start the first leg of my cross-country exercise. I hadn't gone very far when I realized the danger. There were no prominent landmarks to be seen. Very soon I was uncertain of my position and before much longer I was lost. Being in an open cockpit with only light overalls it was fearfully cold and I was soon shivering. I continued under those chilly conditions, hoping to find a pin-point, but was finally overcome with cold and anxiety and forced to land. I chose a large field and landed close to a small farmhouse, maybe fifty feet away.

Bringing the aircraft to a stop, I left the cockpit and went forward to reconnoitre. With the engine still running I sprinted to the cottage door. I was let in by a buxom old woman, about forty I guessed, who somehow recognized my plight and ushered me in towards the large open wood fire. She rushed and served me coffee, always on tap in America, then talked to me. Having gained pertinent information on my whereabouts, I thanked her profusely and left defrosted and warm in less than five minutes. It was snowing steadily again, not heavily but not gently either.

I ran back to the aircraft, quickly strapped in, waved her goodbye and opened the throttle full bore, expecting no problems, but quite unexpectedly a deep and wide sunken ditch

opened up in front of me in the middle of the field. I couldn't
get airborne in time. Nor could I stop, or I would have landed
in it nose first. So with an odd sensation at the bottom of my
stomach, I kept full throttle and hauled back on the stick with
sufficient momentum literally to hop across the gully. The
wheels touched precariously the edge on the other side, but
having full power the aircraft bounced airborne. I was
immediately in control, and confidently set for my next turning
point before heading back to base. I arrived back at the
estimated time of arrival safe and sound. No one was aware of
the unusual event. Should the authorities have found out, I
would have been severely reprimanded, possibly ending up
back in Britain as an air gunner.

I then progressed to more advanced and sophisticated forms
of co-ordination exercises, pulling considerable 'g' forces never
experienced before. Stalls and spins, loops and rolls, upward
turns and rolls of the top on various sequences, ending up with a
simulated engine failure and practice forced landing. Instrument
flying, flying without reference to the visual horizon and
sessions of night flying were introduced at this stage, the
myriads of lights on the first night confusing the mind.

At the end of January 1942 the primary stage of flying with
the open cockpit Stearman was complete. I had a grand total of
seventy-five hours with an above average assessment in my log
book. The basic stage of the course was completed on a Vultee
BT 13A aircraft, a fixed undercarriage monoplane, with a
closed cockpit and a 450 hp engine. The same exercises as at
the primary stage were consolidated, but all manoeuvres were
faster and the navigational trips longer. On completion of basic
training, I totalled 130 flying hours.

During this period I experienced another unusual unrecorded
navigational incident. I had taken off to enjoy a full hour of
aerobatics, in no specific order, but to practise and perfect. I
climbed above the scattered cumulus cloud, cleared my area

Vultee BT 13A: basic trainer with fixed undercarriage

and started the exercises. After a half hour of rolling, diving, looping, spinning in sheer joy, I noticed to my horror that the cloud below had built up considerably and there was little space to see the ground below.

I searched apprehensively for an adequate sized hole, found one to my relief and dived through it fast, before it closed. That was only the beginning of my troubles. The high winds aloft, a common occurrence in Texas, had caused me to drift many miles, and once below I couldn't pin-point my position, as there were no recognizable landmarks. I was utterly lost. I set heading in the general direction of base more in hope than judgement and before long saw a town that I couldn't identify. I was very low on fuel, so there was little alternative but to land and find out where I was.

A massive field lay ahead, so I made a precautionary landing and was immediately alarmed at the rapid sinking of the undercarriage into the light silky soil. I came to a halt abruptly, the aircraft tipping up on its nose but fortunately falling back with a thud the right way up, the wheels sinking lower and lower into the shifting sand.

The cockpit, BT 13A

Revving up, attempting to move forward, the tail bucked once more, the power from the engine sending up large volumes of sandy dust. Throttling back, I looked around in all directions. At first I saw nothing but then from behind in the distance came a large group of about fifty people running towards the aircraft, the men in the vanguard. When they arrived I noted they were all black, men, women and children, the smallest struggling behind. They swarmed around, and stood gazing silently at me in the cockpit. I called one of them up on the wing of the aircraft and asked him the name of the town. He told me Tyler. I informed him I would be taking off immediately, and asked him to tell everyone to stand clear.

However, when I opened up the throttle, it was patently obvious I wasn't going anywhere. The wheels were well and truly stuck; only the tail plane came up along with the dust. My worst fears were realized. Now I was in real trouble, I thought. The people tried to help by dividing themselves into equal numbers and pushing on each wing, but to no avail. Then I had a brainwave. I directed all the helpers to one side and gave orders to push as I revved the engine to full power. The aircraft moved a fraction, slowly at first, bit by bit, turning on its axis. Then it gradually began to move forward and very, very slowly I was picking up speed. I waved goodbye to them all and nonchalantly threw out a few dollars as I moved ahead. They waved me an uncertain farewell.

The field was enormous, but firmed up the further I went. I was moving faster over the hard surface, but was still bumbling along with insufficient air speed towards a high fence that loomed up at the far end of the field. I urged the aircraft forward cursing for more speed, dropped a little flap, used the final ounce of power and at the last second hauled back the stick, pulling the nose up at an alarming angle to stagger clear of the fence. Fortunately I remained airborne, but only just, having barely attained flying speed. I sunk a little but, adjusting the attitude of the aircraft, was able to hold just clear of the ground and so begin a slow climb. Looking at the map and knowing the town I set a heading for the airfield without further incident. I wanted to tell someone about my troubles, but felt apprehensive that it would not remain secret and so decided against it.

During the mid-course break at the end of the primary stage of flying in January 1942, three of us and two unmarried instructors, who coincidentally were friendly rivals at work and play, set off for a fortnight's vacation. The word fortnight is almost unknown to the ordinary American.

Driving south from Dallas we left for the Gulf of Mexico. Passing through Buffalo, we stopped for petrol and refreshment before arriving in Houston. Boarding a bus in Houston I was astonished when someone offered me their fare. In my blue uniform with a white flash on the side cap I had been mistaken for the conductor. America was now at war, the Japs had made their shattering attack on 7 December 1941, and we were allowed to wear uniform.

We arrived in hot, steamy, soporific Galveston later that evening and booked into a hotel. Changing into something cooler, with white shirt and open collar the five of us stepped out and 'did the town'. Ambling around the open harbour, drinking in some sleazy bars, we were back in the hotel by midnight. The two instructors, making all the decisions, summoned room service and promptly booked some female company. Being rather naïve I didn't appreciate what was taking place, but it soon became abundantly clear that it was going to be more than an all night drinking session.

Soon it was my turn to enter the bedroom. I guess I was last, I didn't really know what to expect on arrival so, impelled by curiosity, I opened the door gingerly and stepped inside, closing it quietly behind. She was pale, good looking enough, older than me but no raving beauty. She was naked. Aghast and filled with an inner fear, uncertainty stopped me in my tracks. I noticed at once her high heeled black shoes and flimsy pink underclothes lay on a chair by the window of the dimly lit room. Before this unusual predicament, I had only ever touched a female and had never ever seen anything quite like this before. I looked at her, then looked away as I edged across the room. Turning, I faced her. She raised her head from the pillow and in a pleading voice said: 'What's the matter with you, man? Come on, honey'. I undressed quickly and moved forward tentatively, having to lie on top of her before there was any reaction. It was over quickly, and I was up and dressed and out of the room in a flash. There was some laughter and joking as I got back to the chaps, but I was quietly to remember the details of that first close encounter with a woman.

Driving north from New Orleans to Dallas through the dry state of Texas.
Instructor Howe is just visible, holding a bottle

After this we moved on to New Orleans, Louisiana, and spent a week in what is, in my opinion, America's most interesting city. We went sightseeing daily, promenading with a kaleidoscope of humanity of every race, visiting the historic French quarter, full of graceful ironwork balconies, strolling many times through the shady tree-lined passageways and colourful patios of picturesque Bourbon Street, and along the wide open stretch of famous Canal Street to the riverbank. We sat around in the sun in Jackson Square listening to the beat of traditional jazz and found a few dark bars at infrequent intervals. I regret not taking a steamboat trip up the majestic, shining Mississippi.

During its short existence the BFTS formed a soccer team called The Hurricanes. We played American teams from all over Texas. Soccer in America was in its infancy, and even though we only had four courses to select from, a maximum of 200 students, we were usually well on top. The games were a popular attraction locally.

At the end of the season we met their best combined team from all Texas in the final game of the year at the famous Dallas Cotton Bowl arena. There was a large turnout of spectators, friends and relatives coming from all over the state. With all the publicity many of the local inhabitants came from Dallas and nearby Fort Worth. The game unexpectedly was highly competitive and at the end of the ninety minutes the

No. 1 BFTS 'Hurricanes', champions of the soccer league 1941–2. The picture was taken at the Dallas 'Cotton Bowl'

Football practice, 1942, with the author on the left

score was four goals apiece, so we went on to extra time. During that period I was to give my side victory with a fifth goal, playing forward at the inside right position. The celebrations that followed at the grounds and afterwards were something to experience. No expense was spared, and the fun and games lasted well into the next day.

The other sport I was involved with was ten pin bowling in the local town of Terrell. Bowling wasn't available in Britain in 1941. As an avid participant I soon got the hang of it and became champion of the month. This meant taking on all comers, free of charge for that particular month. Win or lose, the title was then passed on to someone else. Next door to the bowling alley was Mrs Bass's corner drug store. Food and soft drinks were served there and it was well patronized by the boys and the local talent, who flocked in to chat us up. If we couldn't make Dallas at the weekend, it was there at the drug store we passed the time. Mrs Bass was a conspicuously generous person and many of the items we purchased from her drug store had a substantial discount.

American hospitality was boundless in Texas. English visitors to the United States were still not many, so we were unusual and they couldn't do enough for us. When in their company on social occasions it wasn't just a straightforward hello and goodbye, but a much more intense 'You all come back, you all come back', repeated with such sincerity that of course many of us did just that. It was hard to stay away.

Our pay of $28 was spent early on the first long weekend pass at the beginning of the month soon after pay day. The remainder of the month was paid for by gregarious generous American friends with their innate sense of good manners and affection. We did feel guilty accepting all their generosity and being unable to return it, but those marvellous people expected nothing from us except our presence in their company. We must have been pillars of virtue as I recall no antisocial shenanigans with any of our hosts.

Being Scottish with an accent, I was even more uncommon for these southern state Americans. Consequently I was always singled out and found myself the centre of attraction, being encouraged to say something special at parties. Positioning me in a prominent position in the room they would urge me to speak. I

American family hospitality: something they do well

was so consumed with shyness and painfully inarticulate it was embarrassing, but difficult to refuse. I delighted their obsession with Texas, always stating how pleased I was to be there to learn to fly.

They took us driving through the countryside, cities and to parties laid on afterwards when an abundance of food was on display, at which we all gazed with rapture. It took us some days to get used to the sweetness of American food but once acclimatized we ate lustily. On other days we were picked up direct from the camp, taken to their opulent and astonishingly modern air-conditioned homes and delivered back later, many of us having been persuaded to stay overnight.

I revelled in the thrill and deep sensuous pleasure of my physical and mental well-being in this hospitable environment, in the glorious beauty of warm sunny days, and the azure blue sky with the brilliant burning sun on my shoulders. With all that pleasure and good weather, plus exciting flying, money and gorgeous golden beautiful girls, life was idyllic.

One evening three of us were given the use of a large Chevrolet family car. Driving around Dallas we ventured up a one-way street the wrong way and were stopped by the police. Once they had established we were British and under flying training at the nearby aerodrome, they let us go with a few polite words of advice.

On another occasion I spent the night incarcerated in Fort Worth jailhouse. I overstayed my time at a local honky tonk and missed the transport home. Normally we would remain in these night-clubs in Dallas or Fort Worth until the early hours of the morning, enjoying the decadent noisy night-life. There was always someone around to take us home or offer a bed but that night I had overdone it. The police picked me up walking the silent streets, took me to jail, treated me marvellously and drove me back to base in the morning after supplying a hearty breakfast of sausages, bacon and eggs and fresh coffee.

My observations made at the time were that American boys and girls lived a parochial existence and were almost totally ignorant of the outside world. Only a few had ever heard of Glasgow or even Scotland; London, England they did have knowledge of. I noticed that many Americans went to church and that negroes walked on the other side of the street, usually the poor, dark and dowdy, unlit, seamy side. It was also considered a little unsafe to go out walking alone at night. Texans with their overwhelming kindness and their legendary hospitality were a delightful experience. One day I promised myself to return and enjoy the luxury of living in a rich land.

The next unusual navigation event happened at the advanced stage of training. I was now flying the AT6A or Harvard, an aircraft with a 660 hp engine and a retractable undercarriage. 'Do you all fly those big silver ships with no wheels?' was the expression used by the indigenous black population.

I was detailed with others for a long cross-country exercise towards El Paso and back. My aircraft was unserviceable with a

Harvard AT 6A: advanced trainer – 'those big silver ships with no wheels'

minor fault and I didn't take off with the main stream. Immediately I was airborne I was determined to overhaul the last few aircraft, so kept a high power setting and caught up with them at Fort Worth. We proceeded to mix it, roared and soared high over the top of Fort Worth, and when we finished with our short dogfight, set heading to complete the cross-country.

The navigation was straightforward, the weather was good and visibility excellent. I was on my way back, thirty miles south-west of base, feeling good and in control when suddenly my engine stopped. My reaction was instantaneous. I executed a rapid forced landing from 3,000 ft. It was a complete success and I was utterly relieved to make such a safe arrival. I sat for a few moments to recover before I unstrapped and left the cockpit.

Checking the aircraft thoroughly inside and out, I found to my surprise about ten gallons of fuel in the emergency tank. Returning quickly to the cockpit I selected the tank and started the engine. It was a relief to hear it roar. Without more ado I put down optimum flap to reduce my take-off run, held on the brakes, opened up the throttle to full power, released the brakes and took off. I was airborne in an amazingly short run, selected wheels and flaps up with no problem, and landed back at base, thinking all was well. That assumption proved to be ill-founded.

Unfortunately for me some hawk-eyed instructor had seen my aircraft go down and reported the fact that a forced landing had taken place to Air Traffic Control. A fateful bit of malevolence from somewhere on high had been unkind to me.

When I landed and stepped from the cockpit a staff instructor was there to meet me. He told me to report at once to Mr Van Lloyd, the chief flying instructor in his office. Dumping my flying gear and tidying up, I knocked on the door and walked into his office. The chief flying instructor and my squadron commander, in a conciliatory role I hoped, were in discussion when I interrupted. I was not unduly worried.

'You wanted to see me sir, I've just landed,' I said, brightly, but I could tell it was serious. They both looked as black as thunder. It became swiftly apparent there was trouble.

I was on the carpet immediately. The CFI was furious as he roared at me, stating I had committed the cardinal sin by force-landing an aircraft and taking off again, which was strictly against all rules and safety regulations. The fact that I had landed with my wheels down was madness and totally forbidden. He continued with his bristling rhetoric, proceeding with a running commentary on all my previous indiscretions, a surprise to me! His list of my misdemeanours seemed never-ending. He quoted that I had been seen low-flying unofficially and had caused the deputy CFI to chase me halfway across Texas before he could get my aircraft number. Then he had seen me showing off and steep turning off the deck, selecting wheels up before I had sufficient flying speed. I had been reported for completing aerobatics below the minimum safety altitude as prescribed in flying regulations, and he also had reports on my playing about on navigational cross-country exercises. Continuing relentlessly he accused me of disrupting the circuit pattern by cutting in on other aircraft, and went on to list other minor infringements.

He finished by stating he was appalled at my audacity in disobeying all these flying orders; I was suspended from all flying training forthwith. I would never fly under his auspices again. A disagreeable line furrowed the corner of his mouth, as he stated bluntly and unequivocally that I was 'scrubbed'. So ended his verdict, which was shattering. I had remained stoical during his condemnation, but it was only a façade; I was utterly demoralized and in an empiric state of self pity. I had only thirty hours to go to my wings presentation. It was unbearable to contemplate.

I could offer no contradiction but I defended my decision to land wheels down, stating with a note of appeal in my voice that I was not denigrating flying regulations or his authority but saving my life as best I could. If I had crash-landed as recommended, I said, the aircraft would have been unrecoverable and I may well have been killed. At that moment my life was in my hands and I had been confident in my own judgement that I knew how to save it. Regulations or no regulations I would not have done otherwise. That is something I have always adhered to, at crucial moments when my life hung in the balance, never to rely on the muddled indecisive thinking of others.

I continued to put up a spirited defence, objecting strenuously. He listened with attentive patience but it was obvious the decision had already been taken and I had been presented with a decisive *fait accompli*. My plea for mitigation and protestations were to no avail, and I was shattered at the severity of the punishment. I descended into a state of sepulchral gloom and emotional despair. For days, profoundly isolated in my misery, I was a disturbed young man, overcome

Accelerating studies during
suspension

by gloomy forebodings and with a fear of the eventual
outcome.

During my suspension I was allowed to attend ground
school lectures which had kept parallel with our flying and
had reached an advanced level. The standard and manner of
presentation of the subjects by most of our American
instructors was excellent. Their instructional technique,
physical mannerisms and lucid and amusing practical ways
of describing their particular lessons was a pleasure to all in
the classroom. Their wit and fluency abounded, and most
were natural teachers. Of course there was the odd one
whose inadequate possession of the subject and stilted
presentation made matters more tedious by comparison.
Nevertheless, ground school instruction was always eagerly
anticipated.

The RAF was to become final arbiter in my case. They
fought the local verdict and my case was forwarded by special

report to RAF Headquarters at Washington DC. While the case was *subjudice* I was not allowed near the flights, even though I continued with ground school work. I was at the nadir of dejection as I sat meditating silently, disconsolately, alone on my bed in the billets as the flight went flying. It was of paramount importance to me that I became a fighter pilot, so I still harboured a desperate hope that the inquiry would end propitiously and my highest ambitions in life would be fulfilled. To be sent home to the dull life from which I had just escaped; the thought was horrific, but it was a fate that was always a possibility during training. Only success here could obliterate it.

Eventually after about ten days the result of the investigation arrived late one afternoon. The RAF had come to my rescue. I was to be reinstated immediately, training was to continue and to be scheduled so that I finished the course on time with the others. I had a bit of flying to catch up with. That propitious verdict was decreed by chance. The RAF was still very short of pilots and I had been saved by that need, together with my above-average flying grades. I had suffered considerable anxiety, so liberation from the days of suspension was an incredible relief. I yielded to wild exhilaration for the remainder of that evening, being congratulated by the boys on the course on the successful appeal. Suddenly life was very much brighter and I went to sleep easily that night, but it was a pyrrhic victory. The following morning at dispersal I was warned by the Squadron Commander Siebenhausen, his voice dispassionate, that any further misdemeanours would be final curtains. I heeded his words and inwardly resolved to steer clear of any further incidents, sticking rigidly to the straight and narrow path by meticulous observance of the rules, and finish the course.

The final assessment written in my log book by Chief Flying Instructor Van Lloyd was 'Below Average – Breach of Flying

Victory drink

Regulations'. I was still inwardly indignant, considering it manifestly unfair and vindictive. I had already been told I was a natural flyer and my flying grades were mostly above average, so I treated his insipid and fatuous assessment with contempt and obliterated it from my mind at once.

It was a great feeling to have passed the course. The wings presentation and passing out parade was held on 1 May 1942. There was an excited silence as the wings award was made and the badge pinned to the chest. We marched off, resplendent in our blue winged uniforms, the culmination of our ambition and a proud moment for all of us.

I had reached my objective and was now a qualified pilot, having completed a total of 166 flying hours, dual and solo, on three different types of aircraft. With the rank of sergeant I was on the massive pay of 13s 6d per day, a fortune for me. Furthermore, with my natural aggressive temperament and aptitude, I was one of the few selected for Fighter Command,

and would proceed to a life of high adventure at a Fighter Operational Training Unit on my return to the United Kingdom. It was fabulous; I was to become one of wartime's Brylcreem glamour boys! Most went to Bomber Command and a few, who were commissioned, were retained in Canada for instructional duties. Hard luck, I thought. They were unlikely to see any air to air combat unless the war lasted a very long time.

Nearly 75 per cent of our course qualified and a similar amount passed at the other BFTS. Those who failed were sent to Canada either to be trained as navigators or air gunners. Those totally unsuitable, mainly through air sickness, loss of nerve or inability to land without difficulties, were sent directly back to England to become so-called wingless wonders with administrative duties.

CHAPTER 4

Into the Fray

One of the supreme qualities of the young men, few of them over twenty-five, was the light hearted refusal to take either their dangers or their achievements seriously. They had natural buoyancy of spirit which comes with robust youth, perfect health and an adventurous disposition.

The Fight at Odds

We left Dallas late on a beautiful night of a gibbous moon for the long haul north. The homeward journey in a large convoy of fifty ships and more, sailing no faster than the slowest ship, departed from Halifax, Canada early in May 1942. The troopships were packed full of Canadians, soldiers and airmen heading for the war. Temporary friendships were made on the eight day crossing. The Battle of the Atlantic was at its height, and the journey was hazardous.

The convoy was attacked at least half-a-dozen times. German U-boats were now hunting in wolf-packs of up to twenty, invariably through the night. These packs were concentrated in the North Atlantic and this new technique was causing heavy shipping losses to the allied convoys. You could call it Germany's 'happy hour' of the war.

Minutes after one attack, one ship was torpedoed, exploded and sank rapidly, and several more were either stopped or listing so badly that they were unable to continue. The rescue ship at the rear of the convoy, always a dangerous place, steamed to pick up any survivors from the sinking ships while our destroyer, frigate, corvette and cruiser escorts chased around in circles, hooting, signalling and dropping depth charges. That left the convoy temporarily unguarded (except for the odd air patrol), and by the time the escort returned more ships had been sunk, damaged or crippled. News came through that the escort ships had sunk a submarine and another had been damaged. We watched all this going on as we stood on deck at our emergency positions, complete with life jackets. It was fascinating. Those emergency boat drills were persistent throughout the voyage; some were taut with excitement, others were false alarms.

Seas were rough at times on this crossing, ships heeling over many degrees in hurricane-force gales. There was no question, however, of me being sea sick this time around, by now my stomach was used to much more torture than the ship could offer. The incidents certainly helped break up the monotony and created excitement during our long haul back to Britain.

I returned from the United States with an unusual mixture of speech, a concoction of Texan, English and Scottish accent. Imagine a Texas drawl, speaking 'proper' English with a slight Scottish brogue. Except for a few residual Scottish vowels I was informed it sounded Canadian and many took me for that, particularly those who had travelled around. Others didn't have a clue. For the opposite sex I fabricated many stories of my origins, mainly that I came from Kimberley or Johannesburg in South Africa, where the diamonds came from. Many of them believed me and promises made of diamonds paid dividends. When later I returned to Scotland for further flying training, people whom I had left only a year before didn't believe I was a Scot. I was speaking the King's English: 'How Now Brown Cow', not 'Hae noo Broon Coo' made it difficult to convince them of my Scottish origin. When I did prove this, they remarked that if such was the case then I must have swallowed a London apple. I was talking posh.

We arrived at Liverpool and disembarked for a holding unit in England. Many things make travellers glad to get home, a feeling I have experienced many times since. It seems a quiet paradise of green fields and good gardens, of friendliness and cleanliness, security and good order, with life passing at a leisurely comfortable pace. So it was in that summer of 1942, even though there was a war going on. The countryside looked beautiful in the late spring as we made our way to the south coast. It was holiday season when I found myself in Bournemouth. I was billeted in a five star hotel commandeered by the services, awaiting my next flying training posting. There were few parades or inspections and after early morning roll call parade we were set free. Those hours of leisure gave us the opportunity to enjoy ourselves to the full, and we certainly made full use of it, as there were plenty of London girls in town.

In late June I was posted to an advanced flying unit in the Midlands to fly Miles Master aircraft, equivalent in power and performance to the Harvard. It was a refresher and familiarization conversion course in British aircraft and over the British countryside. Navigation was completely different. Gone were the vast, arid fields of Texas, replaced with the patchwork, postage stamp-sized, green fields of England. The towns were not many miles apart but merged into each other, and of course the weather was completely different.

The problems of acclimatization were soon overcome, and after four short trips in the Master I was able to go solo. On a later trip, while on an aerobatic solo trip, my engine suddenly stopped. Fortunately I was high and near enough to go to a subsidiary airfield to execute a successful forced landing. Another pilot doing similar consolidation exercises nearby had no such luck and was killed while practising stalls and spins.

At the end of the course, all pilots proceeding on posting to a Hurricane OTU were converted to and allowed to fly the AFU

Hurricane fighter bomber in action before the coming of the Typhoon (RAF Museum, Hendon)

Hurricane. It was the first aircraft any of us had flown without prior dual instruction; quite a milestone in our flying career.

One hazy September day in 1942 I was duly authorized to fly the Hurricane Mk 1. I climbed into the cockpit to complete a simple thirty minute familiarization exercise. I was briefed not to go into cloud and to avoid the town of Crewe, as there were air balloons positioned above the town. I started the engine and taxied out to the end of the runway, completed all the necessary checks and lined up for take-off. All seemed in order as I eased the throttle fully forward with my left hand to obtain full power. The engine rose to a roar and I was airborne. As I flashed over the end of the runway and pulled the Hurricane into a gentle climbing turn to the left, my difficulties began and it became abundantly clear that I was going to have big trouble.

The nose of the Hurricane dips away from the pilot and it was difficult enough on this first trip to set the correct position and angle of climb relative to the horizon; but if one has other problems when immediately airborne then it becomes a crisis. Hurricane pilots had to transfer the left hand from the throttle lever to the control column, so that the right hand could move a lever on the right of the cockpit to retract the undercarriage.

The aircraft I was flying must have been ancient. The throttle nut had been tightened fully forward with a hammer and chisel. I could see the cut mark. Each time I released my hand from the throttle lever to change hands, the lever slipped back alarmingly, causing the aircraft to lose power rapidly so much so that I was descending sharply instead of climbing. My first attempt was dangerous as I was very close to the ground. It was not possible to tighten the throttle by hand, the hammer had seen to that. That was my predicament, on my first solo in a different type of aircraft and without previous dual instruction. It certainly was a handful.

I tried many times to resolve the situation while the aircraft was yawing, twisting and tipping above and below the horizon in an unbalanced, undulating movement. I was also supposed to be watching where I was going, avoiding cloud and keeping clear of the balloons over Crewe. I sweated profusely trying to sort things out. My head was down in the cockpit. I found myself with the stick between my knees, my feet off the rudders, one hand on the throttle on the left, the other hand on the undercarriage lever on the right, and in cumulus cloud over Crewe. With relief I heard the dull thud from below as the wheels struck home into their bays, but I was still in a precarious situation.

My heart thumped for a moment as I realized my position. With undercarriage up I quickly dived out of the cloud and, with a momentary sense of relief, I turned away from Crewe and its balloons. The perilous little adventure, not entirely of my own making, made me very displeased with the ground staff. I settled the aircraft to normal and returned to base, making my thoughts known to the ground crew on return. Landing was not straightforward either as the flaps didn't work, and I aquaplaned on to sodden grass at the end of the runway. My log book shows that I was airborne exactly thirty minutes. It felt like an eternity.

It dawned on me as I taxied into dispersal that for one reason or another I had been committed to making either a precautionary or forced landing on every aircraft I had flown to date. No damage had been done but I was beginning to wonder over the implications of this menacing trend. I needn't have worried. I suppose the law of averages stood me in good stead and worked in my favour when most needed – during my operational exploits to come.

From my room I glanced anxiously at the falling snow through the frosted windows, wishing it would stop. Much more of it and flying would be cancelled for a week. I wanted to fly the Hurricane again but the thick snow continued to fall. Runways, buildings and trees were soon buried in the stuff. Pulling on my flying boots, donning my brown leather Irvin jacket, I resigned myselt to wait another day and went for breakfast.

The Hurricane OTU was an austerely furnished Nissen-hutted encampment with inadequate heating at a place called Kinnell in the desolate wilds of Fifeshire in Scotland. It was ideal for our requirements. There was nothing other than the weather to distract us from the high intensity flying practices over a period of six weeks, ensuring a proficient and satisfactory standard for the next posting, which would be to an operational fighter squadron.

We flew the full range of formations. They needed rapid and precise corrections of throttle, stick and rudder, and we continually changed positions to obtain the maximum experience. We flew in close VIC formation of three and five aircraft in straight and level flight, progressed to gentle turns, then steep turns, climbing and descending developing into a tail chase and dogfight. We flew in line astern and line abreast, in echelon port and echelon starboard, and unofficially there was a limited amount of formation aerobatics. We also practised battle formation, breaking from these positions to meet the unseen enemy.

We completed air-to-air firing, air-to-ground firing, ciné camera deflection exercises, hooded instrument flying, cloud flying, low flying, and map reading exercises. We also did some night flying using only limited portable lighting equipment. We practised on the link trainer, simulating instrument flying and practising radio beam homings. The anticipatory knack and delicate art of formation flying came easily to me and, with good night vision, night flying was particularly interesting. It was truly an industrious period of intensive flying and, radiant with self confidence, I loved every minute of it.

It was at Kinnell, the satellite aerodrome of the OTU, twenty miles distant from Dundee, that we were subjected to the decompression chamber. We sat in a specially prepared mobile vehicle, and were taken up in stages six at a time, with and without oxygen, to a simulated maximum altitude of 42,000 ft, then made rapid descents at an average rate of over 4,000 ft per minute. We remained at high levels of over 30,000 ft for a period of fifteen minutes. A few pilots had 'bends' from the effects of gas expansion, some were rendered anoxic at maximum altitude, while others had slight ear or sinus troubles during the descent. Others had a combination of all the symptoms, but very rarely did anyone fail this test completely, certainly not enough to be taken off flying. Most suffered no ill effects.

We finished the course towards the end of November and then excitedly awaited our postings to a front line fighter squadron. There was no choice of posting. Most pilots wanted the superb Spitfires, but I was particularly happy and content to be posted to a new Typhoon Squadron forming at Edinburgh. I hurriedly packed my kit and set off for my new appointment.

I left the OTU with a total of 270 flying hours, ready, willing and desperate to join the fray before it was all over. I would have wished to be nearer to the enemy and join an active squadron on the south coast of England, but mine was a good posting and I was entirely satisfied. I knew we would be heading south soon enough.

I flew operations at Tangmere,
War base and home for me,
Horizons wide, with hidden fear,
Flying low o'er insatiable sea.

Airfield my home and fighter base,
Scarred in battle by enemy hate,
Aircrew of youthful carefree face,
Rendezvous with war and fate.

Our pastimes were spent at dispersal,
Some days with little to do,
Operations more than rehearsals,
Left us sadly minus a few.

The missions forever were thrilling,
The adrenalin milling around,
The furious flak ever killing,
Bombs away and homeward bound.

They awaited with patience on standby,
Keen and ready to fly,
To seek and find the enemy,
Some to live, some to die.

The Typhoon, no ordinary aircraft,
Not only by action but name,
Cleaving the skies with powerful zest,
Now stands in the Hall of Fame.

CHAPTER 5

Tangmere

The Typhoon, the largest fighter designed during the Second World War, entered operational service with the RAF in early 1942. A fighter initially, it became a fighter-bomber, airfield strafer, train buster, tank destroyer, anti-shipping strike aircraft, and proved excellent as a support machine for ground forces. Such was the Hawker Typhoon Fighter-Bomber, a massive new fighter weighing 7 tons. Over 3,000 were built in Gloucester between 1941 and 1945.

It seems almost inconceivable that this famous aeroplane was almost abandoned at the beginning of its career as a total failure. The crisis came about through fitting the Napier Sabre twenty-four cylinder engine to the aircraft while the new engines were still in the process of development, with teething troubles galore. Numerous other faults gave cause for concern and doubt about the Typhoon. Structural weaknesses were found in the rear of the fuselage both at early testing stage and later when the first service machines flew with squadrons. Difficulties were encountered in the ammunition feed mechanism for the 20 mm cannons, and the carbon monoxide fumes escaped into the cockpit. The disappearance of several Typhoons on early operations was later attributed either to one or a combination of these faults. Another factor causing concern was the poor performance of the Typhoon at higher altitudes. Its maximum speed was just over 400 mph at about 20,000 ft but that fell rapidly at greater heights. 30,000 ft plus saw Typhoons hanging on their propeller at a speed of only 160 mph and almost ready to fall out of the sky.

'Achtung Typhoon'

TYPHOON
The violent mythological father of the winds
The storm was brewing, soon the Typhoon would come.

The aircraft had been designed as a replacement interceptor fighter for the ubiquitous Hurricane, even before that rugged and resourceful plane was in service in any great numbers. But thanks to the efforts of aviation and service personnel, the Hawker Typhoon eventually began to show much more promise and was found to be very effective particularly below an altitude of 20,000 ft. It was continuously and extensively modified and improved. Subsequently it blossomed into one of the most formidable weapons of the day and became the best ground and interdiction attack plane of the Second World War. Events decreed that the Typhoons would take their place in the Hall of Fame.

A new German single seater fighter that suddenly appeared on the scene changed everything in the Typhoon's favour. The Focke-Wulf FW 190 outclassed and outgunned the Spitfire V and the Hurricane II and looked like being a king-sized problem in the air war over France and the Low Countries. It was also capable of making quickfire hit and run raids on southern

England. This led to further rapid development programmes on the Typhoon in an effort to meet the new menace. It was an uphill task, but was eventually justified by the Typhoon's success against the Focke-Wulf FW 190 in combat.

Other difficulties still remained. It was found that some aircraft did not come out of dives to attack these German fighters and other ground targets. The tail unit broke away and pilots died not knowing the cause. This particular weakness was overcome by riveting butt strap plates around the tail fuselage joints. Out of the first 150 Typhoons delivered to the RAF over one hundred were involved in accidents attributed to failures of either the new engine or airframe.

The Typhoon, affectionately known as the 'Tiffy', now changed its fighter role to act as one of the most deadly accurate attack planes used by the Allies during the war. When fitted with underwing rocket projectiles, no other weapon proved so effective. The aircraft came into its own and made history. Some pilots weren't too happy in this role, but nevertheless they operated it to deadly effect on enemy coastal shipping in cross-Channel low level sweeps, creating havoc among German E-boats, coastal vessels, flak ships and minelayers in the English Channel.

Inland, the rocket-firing Typhoons blasted enemy airfields, trains and bridges, destroying large concentrations of men and armour, radar installations and gun emplacements. Anything of military value was attacked and destroyed. Train busting in particular became a Typhoon speciality.

When the invasion of Europe was imminent, there was a build up of the Second Tactical Air Force, and by D-Day, 6 June 1944, more than twenty squadrons of the RAF were equipped with the lethal and terrifying Tiffies. They played a major role in the beach-head invasion plans. In Normandy Typhoons became famous for the devastating attacks on German infantry and armour, particularly in the Argentan and

Falaise Gap where rocket-firing and bomb carrying Typhoons wrought havoc on bridges and blocked many escape routes.

The activity of Typhoons, rocket and bomber, was said by the German army staff to be well nigh unendurable, for the morale of the troops was adversely affected by the continuous onslaught of the attacks. Typhoons operated a 'Cab Rank' close support technique. An RAF liaison officer on the ground, usually a pilot, would call down waiting airborne aircraft patrolling at about 10,000 feet to attack convenient targets with pinpoint accuracy. They would dive with all guns blazing. This gave great help to the Allied forces in heavy combat on the beach-head close to the bomb line. That close support role was commonplace on the beach-head until the eventual breakthrough at Caen.

After the collapse of Caen, squadrons of Typhoons continued on the rampage, attacking German troops and vehicles trying to extricate themselves from the Falaise Gap, Argentan and beyond. They attacked several enemy army headquarters further inland, resulting in their total destruction. Other vital targets were continually pounded as the offensive moved east.

I joined No. 197 Typhoon Fighter Squadron during the first week of December 1942 at RAF Drem, East Lothian. The squadron had been formed on paper by the authority of an Air Ministry Order at RAF Turnhouse Aerodrome, near Edinburgh in late November. No aircraft were delivered to Turnhouse as the move to Drem occurred a few days later, and it was there the new Typhoons were sent intermittently during the cold wet months of December and January.

The new Squadron badge was of a lion's jamb holding a sabre, representing strength and power and the squadron motto was *Findimus Caelum*, 'we cleave the sky'. Both were

Squadron crest: 'we cleave the sky'

acknowledged as very appropriate for the new squadron's aircraft and its new pilots.

Drem, situated some 20 miles east of Edinburgh, was a small grass aerodrome, sloping unevenly from north-west to south-east. It was a little hilly and bumpy with some soft patches particularly during the winter months. The airfield had been used initially as a decoy and dummy aerodrome during the Battle of Britain, when it had been equipped with the latest airfield lighting system. This system was installed later at many other RAF aerodromes and became known as the 'Drem system' to all RAF personnel.

I arrived at the wooden huts that were the squadron dispersal on a sleeting windy morning on 1 December 1942. There were a number of brand new Typhoon aircraft standing nearby, canopies and engines hooded, without markings, turned into wind and tied down because of the gale. The place looked deserted, cold and silent. Not a soul was visible. I wondered if I had come to the right place. It was a bleak outlook and I concluded there would be no flying for some time.

Reporting inside I was warmly welcomed by the incumbent commanding officer, a Belgian, and a flight commander, and told I was the third member of the squadron to arrive. After some pleasantries I was informed there was much preparation and administrative work to be done in a short space of time. We worked assiduously during the next two weeks, setting up offices, positioning furniture and flying lockers, arranging maps and charts on the walls of the dispersal crew rooms of both flights.

The pilots and aircraft continued to arrive, and by mid-December we had almost a full complement of men and machines, pilots and ground crew. The aim now was to attain operational status for the squadron as quickly as possible.

The pilots were a mixed bunch. We had three exuberant wise-cracking Canadians (one of them lies buried in Tangmere churchyard), three modest gentle Belgians, two quiet New Zealanders, two likeable plain Poles, one Southern Irishman, charismatic, fair-haired and smiling, full of the usual blarney, who would surely have been rapidly promoted had he lived. We also had two tough, extrovert, loquacious Australians, with the verbal delivery of a machine gun enough for any British squadron. More than two ebullient Australians in any one squadron and they began to take over! We kept our two in different flights. Sometimes their flamboyance and bluntness caused frustration among others. The remainder of the pilots were British, English, Scots and one Welshman. With a doctor, adjutant, engineering and intelligence officer, a total of forty of us were available for the first squadron photograph.

As we got to know one another better over the weeks, the personalities in this cosmopolitan crowd became a good foil for one another and a feeling of camaraderie and *esprit de corps* quickly developed. Chicanery was on a relatively small scale, mainly caused by unequal amounts of flying time and operational sorties, both of which we wanted more of. Nevertheless an unrivalled comradeship developed over the months and years, something that would never occur again.

It was then three weeks since I left OTU and, not having flown for such a lengthy period and being relatively inexperienced, I was checked out on a Master aircraft specially allocated to the squadron for this purpose. A quick trip with the flight commander was necessary before being set loose on the fearsome Typhoon. We worked on a first come first served basis and since I was first to arrive on the squadron I was first to be checked out and first to fly. All the other pilots followed suit in due course.

Pilots' notes had been studied at length in conjunction with numerous cockpit checks, some being carried out blindfolded. I was absolutely familiar with the cockpit drills and felt confident as I signed the various certificates of proficiency and

The original members of 197 Typhoon squadron, which was formed in
December 1942 at Drem, East Lothian, Scotland. The ticks indicate those
who survived the war; the crosses those who weren't so lucky

Pilot's Order Book for the fuel, hydraulic, electrical and communication systems and engine.

I first flew the Typhoon Mark 1a with the car door-type hood on 20 December 1942, some nine months after it had entered service with the RAF. Completing the external checks, I vividly remember the exalted feeling as I climbed fully kitted into the cockpit. I wore a white silk scarf on that occasion (my other scarf was red, spotted white), cream chamois leather gloves over an inner pair of silk ones, black sheepskin-lined flying boots, and light blue flying overalls under a yellow waistcoated 'Mae West' life jacket with a parachute and rubber dinghy.

The pilot sat high in this big fighter. I stepped in and settled on the hard dinghy base attached to the parachute, which fitted into the steel bucket seat of the cockpit. I strapped myself in, clipped on the face mask, plugged in the RT, and switched on the oxygen. With its long powerful looking nose, three large prominent propeller blades, thick strong apparent anhedral/dihedral wings, wide undercarriage and four evenly spaced, threatening thrusting cannons, the Typhoon conveyed to me an impression of power and brute strength.

When finally settled and feeling at ease, I started the 2,200 hp engine with a bang. The starting procedure could be temperamental. The twenty-four cylinder Napier Sabre engine was provided with a Coffman starter used in conjunction with a Kigas primer. The amount of priming required depended on the engine temperature and it was imperative to get the combination right for the engine to start first time. When the starter switch was operated the engine would fire and spring to life with a loud explosion, causing clouds of acrid heavy exhaust smoke to stream out from either side of the engine. The smoke then quickly thinned and disappeared as the engine warmed up with an even roar. Unscrewing the control, I primed the engine with the required number of strokes and started first time. I spent a few minutes checking that

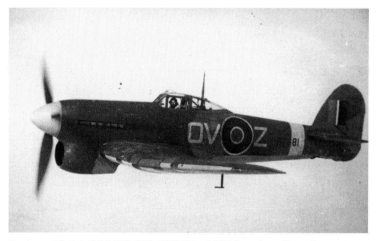

Typhoon Mk 1A (12 M/C) OV–Z R7681 of 197 Squadron, flown by me at Drem, in December, 1942

temperature and pressure were normal. Noting all was well and retightening the primer, I waved chocks away to the ground crew awaiting my signal, released the brakes, rolled forward, checked the brakes operated and taxied slowly out for take-off. I could sense the hidden power of this new Napier Sabre engine.

Full of tension and excitement, cautiously edging forward, I called the control tower for take-off clearance. I swung the nose into the wind and lined up this plane with the awesome reputation on the runway. Positioning dead centre, quickly completing the cockpit checks, and revving the engine to clear it, I held hard on the brakes, then slowly released them and gradually opened up the throttle to maximum take-off power.

On take-off, as the stick was pushed forward and the tail unit lifted, there was an unpleasant tendency for the aircraft to swing to starboard. This inherent swing could develop into a highly critical situation with eventual loss of control if application of the port rudder wasn't anticipated. Many examples of the late application of rudder were witnessed as we watched inexperienced pilots struggle for control. There were some hairy take-offs. Being aware of this inbuilt idiosyncrasy I gently fed on a fraction of port rudder very slightly before the tail unit was fully up, which neutralized the tendency, and the swing never materialized. Having accomplished a straight take-off I used this technique continually, and was to have little trouble during my tour on 'Tiffies'.

The powerful engine then surged to a massive roar as I hurtled down the runway, quickly gaining flying speed. I rapidly checked all instruments, intently confirming everything was functioning well, eased the control column back and was airborne, climbing away rapidly. I was surprised at the ease of take-off. Quickly selecting wheels up and the small amount of flap I used to offset unnecessary undercarriage strain on the bumpy runway, noted the green indicator lights go on and then out indicating undercarriage up, and settled the aircraft in the climb at the recommended speed of about 300 mph.

The intoxicating feeling of power and speed was marvellous and I quickly found myself at a high altitude and levelling out. Flying around for some minutes at about 20,000 feet, getting the feel of the aircraft and clearing the local area, I then proceeded to take the aircraft and myself to our respective limits.

I completed the sequence of aerobatics, stalls, slow rolls, loops, upward rolls, incipient spins and some barrel rolls on the way down. I found all the manoeuvres easy to perform but sustained high gravitational loads not experienced before. The thrust of 6G pushed my sagging jaw and chin down to my chest, and inexorable centrifugal force drove my blood ever downwards from my brain into my boots, my vision greying and my legs feeling like leaden weights. By easing the controls, in seconds I could return to normal if and when it became too hard to bear. Satisfied with this work out, I made a very propitious assessment of this exciting aircraft's performance as I headed back to base to complete a couple of circuits and landings, made relatively easy now that I knew my aircraft better.

On returning to the circuit, slowing down to a landing configuration, I carried out a normal continuous curved approach with wheels down and locked, then with full flap selected I turned on to short finals. A normal fighter aircraft approach, only this one was a little faster than most other aircraft at the time. The ground rushed up that much quicker. The approach speed in the turn was between 120 and 130 mph gradually reducing to 95–100 mph and further still when rounding out for touchdown at 75 mph. This standard approach, however, was not always the procedure adopted, and many variations whether or not intentional were performed when rejoining the circuit for landing. Much depended on the skill, daring and exuberance of the individual.

I landed safely, and quickly completing the after landing checks without stopping, taxied back to dispersal, exhilarated and feeling pleased with the thirty minute flight. Stepping from the cockpit, I jumped to the ground among eager faces awaiting my arrival; all were anxiously awaiting their turn.

'How did it go?' they asked.

'Marvellous,' I said, giving the thumbs up. 'A piece of cake.'

Explaining the details of the trip to those around me, from take off to landing, I then signed the authorization book, DCO, duty carried out. The Typhoon, so long awaited to fly, had been conquered and what a magnificent machine it was! I was going to be lucky enough to fly it on operations.

Even allowing for all the bad winter weather and the Christmas break, all pilots were soon converted to type. It was a matter of building up flying hours. This was accomplished by squadron formations, flights formations, practising interceptions, air-to-air and air-to-ground ciné camera attacks, dogfights and a small amount of night flying by moonlight to ensure the squadron obtained operational status as quickly as possible.

On these early squadron formations the difficulties in starting the engines were soon evident. With failure of the first cartridge, the second and then the third and final cartridge would be fired, which meant that reloading was necessary if the engine did not start. So it would happen that several Typhoons would be left banging away at dispersal while the remainder of the squadron taxied out for take-off. The pilots who were left behind left the cockpit in a flaming temper as they lost yet another trip. Experience on type helped in selecting the correct inversely proportional combination of strokes for engine temperature. Four strokes of Kigas priming pump for a very cold engine, diminishing in numbers with an increase in temperature, was the rule of thumb used. It didn't always click.

The squadron became officially operational in late January 1943 but there was little likelihood of enemy activity in these parts, until one day the unexpected happened. I was on standby readiness when the scramble came through. A JU 188 was reported approaching the east coast at a high altitude. My senses tingled as I dashed for the cockpit, jumped in, strapped up quickly with the aid of the mechanics and taxied out fast. Turning on to the runway without stopping I opened up the throttles and went roaring down the runway at full bore. I was so keen to get airborne and give chase that I purposely selected wheels up before I actually had flying speed. I sank a little as I banked hard left into a tight turn, felt a tug momentarily but nothing registered on the instruments in the cockpit, so I climbed away at maximum speed. My number two caught me up and we settled in the climb, flying line abreast and taking headings from the control tower, soon reaching 30,000 feet. Proceeding on an easterly heading we scanned the sky, peering with a predatory eye at the broad horizon for a black speck that could be the enemy. I turned the gun button to ready, checked the gun sight in eager anticipation of feeling the fire of four 20 mm cannons and waited, but nothing happened. Suddenly over the radio came the bad news: return to base, the enemy had disappeared – a common occurrence at this latitude, and an anti-climax.

It was a bright clear sunny day, with only a little cirrus and broken cirrostratus above us. We were both still excited with the scramble activities so decided to have a bit of fun on our return. After completing a few individual aerobatics, we engaged in a dogfight on the descent before I broke away to indulge in a whim of the moment. Acting rather capriciously and ignoring the likely consequences, I took the liberty of beating up the airfield.

I selected the squadron dispersal and set the Typhoon into a power dive at full throttle. There was some vibration and stiffening of the controls as I approached the fantastic speed of 500 mph. Continuing down to zero feet I flashed over the squadron 'B' flight dispersal at roof-top level. I kept low, pulling hard on the stick, turned to make another attack on the dispersal before running in for a break and landing. It was an exciting and exhilarating trip.

Taxiing in and switching off, thinking no more about the beat up, I was informed the Commanding Officer requested my presence. I marched in. It seemed I'd rattled his ornate inkwell and it had slipped off the corner of his desk, spoiling his carpet. Leaving his office I was informed by the Flight Commander that I had taken a couple of inches off the propeller blades. That, I thought, accounted for the sharp tug on taking off and possibly the vibration on the dive. I explained to the Engineering Officer that I'd hit the bank at the end of the runway on take-off, felt a short sharp jerk, and somehow the two inches must have been chopped off then.

No disciplinary action was taken by the CO. But his face expressed a certain gravity as he said that I was tempting providence too far to carry on in this manner. He was right, as later that day another pilot decided to do a slow roll on his return. With his excess speed from the dive and insufficient nose-up altitude when upside-down he couldn't hold enough forward pressure on the control column and nose-dived inverted into the airmen's quarters on the domestic site. He had no hope of survival. Fortunately no one except himself was killed.

The squadron was ordered to move south. Now officially classified as fully operational, we were ready, willing and thirsty for combat. There were raptures of enthusiasm all round and undisguised jubilation that evening at a spontaneous party, always the best type I thought, when we were informed of our destination.

However, directly before the move something quite tragic and totally unexpected happened to give us all a severe jolt. Flying training was taking place as normal, many aeroplanes taking off and landing. Some of us were outside dispersal when an aircraft overflying the airfield at about 2,000 feet before joining the circuit for landing, suddenly broke in two. The entire tailplane had fallen off the Typhoon. The aircraft dived vertically and exploded at the end of the airfield, the tailplane landing simultaneously nearby. There was a moment of dazed silence. We were stunned by the catastrophe, and general gloom and fear surrounded the flight office. There was obviously no chance of survival for the pilot. We hoped for a miracle but knew he could not be alive. We feared he would be so awfully burnt and mangled we would not recognize him, and our worst fears were realized. He was buried with full military honours. Yet again a Typhoon tail had taken its inevitable toll.

At the subsequent emergency inquiry it was assumed that the pilot's neck was broken at the moment of the fatal fracture, such was the rapid abrupt dive of the fuselage as the tailplane fell away. Beechy was the squadron's first fatality, but many more were envisaged as the squadron became operational. He was a tall, pleasant, softly spoken, smiling character who was well liked by everyone. They were not crocodile tears I shed in private over my friend. I vowed to myself never to make any more truly close friends for the remainder of the war.

The advance party had left by rail as we flew south a day or so after the unhappy event, an uneasy feeling foremost in all our minds. It was a relief to land for refuelling at RAF Duxford, where the first Typhoon squadrons were formed, and then again at our destination airfield on the south coast. Each aircraft was flown away to be modified and the tailplane strengthened. We were now gradually being equipped with the Typhoon Mk 1B whose sliding hood gave us much appreciated all-round vision.

The squadron flew into RAF Tangmere, near Chichester, late in March 1943. The next day the main and rear parties arrived by rail and road from Scotland. The squadron move was complete. Now in an operational capacity much nearer the war, we were all anticipating the exciting days that lay ahead. Tangmere, a maximum activity station since the Battle of Britain, was to be my operational base for the next year and a half. I loved it, the most action-packed, exhilarating and crucial period of my life; one that lives vividly with me.

On arrival we formed a 'wing' with No. 486 New Zealand Squadron already based there. With Spitfire squadrons at the satellite aerodromes of Westhampnett and Merston, and with a special operating unit of Westland Lysanders engaged in clandestine work functioning in one corner of the airfield, the area was an exceedingly active flying complex. Aircraft were coming and going from dawn to dusk. Additional night flying and secret operations occurred at infrequent intervals. The well-decorated pilots and observers of that specialist unit operated on pre-arranged nightly visits to somewhere in Nazi-occupied France, sometimes with the underground resistance movement of the Marquis. The unit was forever changing personnel; only a thin faint pencilled line in the mess ledger indicated those who failed to return.

Our time of arrival coincided with low level daylight raids by Focke-Wulf 190s along the south coast. This had brought the Hawker Typhoon squadrons as a counter measure to Tangmere, Manston and other stations in the south of England. The Tiffies acting in an offensive role from these stations had great success against hit and run raiders. Later, with further development and more effective weapons, they created havoc throughout northern France. Those were the two roles which immortalized the Typhoon, and I was lucky enough to be involved. It was a fighter pilot's dream come true.

Tangmere was a permanent aerodrome, and one of the best fighter bases of the war. It had been an integral part of the Battle of Britain air defence system, and was an active airfield from the beginning of the Second World War. It had been constructed and opened during the latter part of the First World War and operational squadrons had arrived there before proceeding to France just before Armistice Day. Early in 1919 the airfield closed, but was retained by the Air Ministry and reopened in 1925. It remained much the same until 1937 except for a new officers' mess built in 1930. With the expansion of the RAF the aerodrome itself was expanded and the grass airfield was converted to an aerodrome with two concrete runways and new buildings. The reconstruction and conversion was completed in August 1939.

Tangmere was a practical fighter unit and also a Sector Headquarters of No. 11 Fighter Group. The base had control

Pilots of 'B' Flight at Tangmere, 1943. Note the car-door type hood fitted with wind-down windows, which restricted pilots' vision

over many other fighter units at nearby airfields in addition to its own squadrons. The squadrons had been responsible for the air defence of London and the south-east coast of England during the Battle of Britain, and had earlier provided air cover during the evacuation of British Expeditionary Force from Dunkirk.

Tangmere was severely bombed in August 1940; damage was immense. Two large hangars and othe installations were totally destroyed, but miraculously the aerodrome capability was hardly affected. The large force of Junkers JU 87 dive-bombers had caused a great deal of destruction in a successful attack. But repairs were rapid. Tangmere came into prominence again when providing air cover for the ill-fated Dieppe raid in August 1942. It remained very active until after D-Day, controlling and directing a large part of the fighter cover for the Normandy landings. Tangmere also provided aircraft to combat

Tangmere village memorial stone
near the Military Aviation Museum

the new V1 rockets, which were arriving over the south-east coast bound for London.

Many famous figures visited Tangmere. Celebrities like Lord Trenchard, General Dwight Eisenhower, General de Gaulle, Anthony Eden, Lord Mountbatten, Lord Tedder, and on one occasion the entire cast of the Windmill Theatre. Other screen and stage personalities passed through. The King and Queen visited Tangmere in July 1944, when a royal investiture was conducted and awards were made to station personnel. (After the successful landings in Normandy, the aerodrome reverted to a non-operational role and remained with the Ministry of Defence until finally closed in October 1970. So much has been thought of the airfield over the years that it now has a band of dedicated devotees who have established a Tangmere Aerodrome memorial museum. A memorial stone has been erected to this most famous of aerodromes.)

There was a large private residence situated just outside the main gate not far from the sergeants' mess. The house, with its colourful and pleasant gardens that proliferated with honeysuckle, carnations, azaleas and a wealth of roses, whose intoxicating perfumes periodically pervaded every corner of the house. It was to be my home until the squadron moved to a temporary landing ground before D-Day, a year later. It was well furnished, always warm and comfortable. We were two to a room with some limited batting service. Living in that house will remain for me one of the happiest times of the war. The friendships, the triumphs we shared, the spontaneous parties and hilarious nocturnal activities, the sound of raucous laughter and bursts of song made it a marvellous abode. We were full of vim and vigour, always talking shop, although time was spent in a frivolous manner when not on duty.

The noise generated after a successful sortie was incredible, everyone excitedly shouting around their own particular story. Some nights after a heavy booze-up, happily intoxicated and feeling hungry, we fortified ourselves by surreptitiously pinching bread and onions from the mess, and creeping back home with our loot, quietly and stealthily entering the house so as not to wake those on dawn patrol. Trying to cook toast and onions on a small electric portable grill, jovially half pissed, and at the same time be quiet, is not easy. Our endeavours caused much laughter, and with the use of utensils and the inevitable clatter of noise we often woke up the household. The result was that on another day when it was your turn to be asleep, others reciprocated.

The squadron's first operational sorties from Tangmere consisted mainly of defensive and intercept standing patrols carried out some two to five miles from the coast. Our allotted area, covered in sections, stretched from as far east as Beachy Head to the southernmost part of the Isle of Wight at St Catherine's point, and on round to The Needles in the west.

Hourly patrols took place from dawn to dusk daily. In the long hot summer days, subject to weather conditions, that meant from 5 a.m. to 10 p.m. If you were on the dawn patrol you were up so early it was still dark; this patrol usually lasted double time, enabling the relief pilots to have a longer bedtime. It was always a pleasure to spot the relief aircraft arriving on that early stint. On returning from the dawn patrol, having enjoyed the first beams of sunrise, it was possible to pick mushrooms which grew prolifically on parts of the airfield before wandering back to the mess for a big breakfast.

Flying these repetitive defensive patrols could be monotonous and boring to some pilots, a monotony that threatened to be dangerous because of lack of concentration. To me though it was low flying at 300 mph and I was forever optimistic that at any second I'd receive an exciting vector from Air Traffic Control. Patrols could be highly dangerous because flying in atrocious weather conditions over the sea at low level made it easy to misjudge height with little or no horizon. You could easily become disorientated without visual horizon. Constant reference to cockpit instruments was a necessity, otherwise loss of orientation creating an unusual position might mean you could slip unobtrusively into the sea. Some losses were caused by this uncanny phenomenon. Concentration was also needed to avoid cliff tops. We tended to close in to keep visual contact as the weather worsened. We had to avoid the odd balloon dotted intermittently along the coast, search and scan the horizon for enemy hit-and-run raiders and be wary of suspicious friendly aircraft; but the worst of all was losing sight of each other in the turn. Those risks together with a suspect engine could make an hourly patrol anything but boring.

To keep ourselves occupied and active in periods of very good weather conditions we would dare one another to get as low to the waves as possible. Looking at each other, judging

Passing the time between sorties. The bikes at the rear were our main mode
of travel between billets, mess and dispersal

height, we would in turn slowly but surely edge our way down
foot by foot towards the turbulent sea, so that our propellers
were just clipping the waves. We had to beware of 'white
horses'. Only occasionally would we be alerted by Air Traffic
Control and sent after a penetrating enemy hit-and-run raider or
dispatched for some other investigation. Such tasks were
always welcome and you were considered lucky if it happened
during your hourly commitment.

Sometimes lack of activity and inclement weather combined
precluded all movement. At other times the sun shone but still
there was no flying. We were sometimes 'browned off' at
having to maintain a state of readiness at dispersal, then sit in
the cockpit on standby readiness. Time was only punctuated
with eventless patrols during a long day. Pilots passed the time
during these periods playing the inevitable game of cards.
There was always pontoon or a rubber at a bridge school; or we
played chess, caught up with some sleep, wrote, read or

stretched out on the cool grass idly watching the flying going on or sunbathing. Two of us, or four if enemy activity warranted it, sat sweltering in the sun tightly strapped in the hot oven of our cockpits looking with envy at those lazing about. Soon it would be our turn to get out of the hothouse, unless of course we were lucky enough to be scrambled.

It was at dispersal where the squadron pilot spent most of his time on duty. Dispersal was also often the last place he saw on earth. It was there that all the camaraderie and *esprit de corps* developed, though at times minor skirmishes and frustrations were evident. I was then a flight sergeant earning the grand sum of 15*s* 6*d* per day. Some pilots complained of meagre pay but it was never of any significance to me. I clearly remember visiting Chichester one afternoon with my savings. £50 in notes in my wallet made me feel relatively rich. Ready cash was available, as airmen in those days didn't have a bank account, but were paraded for their pay. Not till I was commissioned in 1944 did I have a bank account.

Rex Mulliner was the flight commander of 'B' flight – above average height, good looking, with fair hair. He had a small droopy fair moustache, slightly saffron with nicotine. He was a smooth, amiable, mild-mannered English gentleman, four years older than myself. I liked him from the moment of our introduction. No bullshit here I thought; a man I could work for. My prediction and premonitions proved to be correct. He never abused his power or authority, but was a pleasant and persuasive personality. He was always firm but fair, with an inbuilt capacity for obtaining the most beneficial returns from everyone under his command.

I was to appreciate his leadership, his didacticism and other endearing qualities which merited respect, over our protracted

Rex Mulliner (Imperial War Museum)

tour together. He chaperoned my first operational flight. He was my guide, philosopher and friend when I needed him, and if he wasn't the most dashing of fighter pilots his steadfastness and professional sangfroid contained my exuberance in the early days of operations. It undoubtedly contributed to saving my life.

He was a man who knew that the elements of command do not go beyond sound common sense. I cannot help contrasting this likeable man with the peripheral figure of a squadron commander with less endearing qualities. On a nonsensical whim he would make all of us, including the officers but not himself, don their full flying kit including parachute, and run around the dispersal area. Squadron morale was high until he came along, but we harboured an implacable hatred for him, as he was such an arrogant pompous ass. Fortunately, he didn't last too long, and our morale rose when he was posted. In my judgement he was a typical example of how not to use power and authority. There were more like him during my long career in the service, as there are in other walks of life. I was always scornful of such stupid men in positions of authority. My impulsive tongue and tactlessness never did pay dividends, but to me, to be direct, unswervingly honest and truthful was a way of life.

Rex Mulliner will always be remembered for an incident that happened in the corridor of the officers' mess at Tangmere one evening. Rex and some others grabbed the Queen Bee in the passageway, stripped her bum bare and nailed her knickers to the ceiling. That head WAAF was a severe-looking character, and a poor sport who didn't take kindly to the spirited high jinks of the young men. She made a full report of the evening's antics to the Station Commander next morning. The investigation was, however, contained at station level and the incident was closed, much to the relief of Rex and the others.

It was to Rex, one day in 1943, that I whispered I was unable to drive. I considered it paradoxical that I could fly a Typhoon but couldn't drive a car, but also prudent that he should know in order to avert any embarrassment should he call upon me in an emergency. I eventually taught myself to drive in a squadron jeep at Lübeck in Germany two years later.

Rex, Len Richardson and myself were to be the only three pilots from the original members of the Flight to last the full eighteen months' operational tour. We left the squadron within days of one another. It is sad to report that Rex, like Len, having survived the dangers of combat, was killed after the war – in his case in a civilian flying disaster when, as captain of a civil airliner, he crashed and all aboard were killed. I am now the sole survivor of the original 'B' Flight.

The squadron taxied out for take off, red section of 'A' Flight first, followed by yellow section. Next came 'B' Flight, blue section followed by green. The twelve Typhoons moved forward along the runway, sections equally spaced, slowly gathered speed, control columns stiffening, tails up. Pulling back on the stick we were then airborne, jostling for position, pumping throttle back and forth endeavouring to stay close with each other. It was difficult, hot and dangerous, with all of us juggling to stay in position in the bumpy conditions created by other aeroplanes' slipstreams while turning low over the tree tops.

Straightening up and coasting outbound, I took a last look at the white cliffs as the squadron turned south across the halcyon water. It was a beautiful sunny day. There wasn't a cloud in the sky and scarcely a breath of wind. Our fast moving dark shadows were cast flat on the shiny surface of the sea.

It was early in April 1943 that I actually crossed the French coast and became truly operational. I looked out through the cockpit canopy, down from 10,000 ft and glimpsed the breakers along the coastline of the European continent for the very first time. The target was a dive-bombing attack on a place called Tricqueville near Dieppe.

I wondered what my end might be. Would I be shot down this moment by flak or enemy aircraft? If so, would I be shot dead on sight or taken prisoner of war; or would I be lucky enough to escape and contact the escape and evasion underground movement? 'Where are the enemy fighters?' 'Where is the felonious Hun?' 'Where is this flak coming from?' Such were my random thoughts as we changed formation to echelon starboard on the run up to the target. It was a little nerve-racking to think that at any moment, and if unlucky, I could be blasted out of the sky.

The power dive went exceedingly well amid light and heavy flak, even though it was disconcerting and distracting to glimpse all those little black puffs of cloud that suddenly appeared in front of the windscreen. It was a relief to bomb, break away and pull up to rejoin the squadron out of the danger that encircled us. Soon we had re-formed and were heading back to England. It had been an odd feeling, diving down, hanging into the cockpit straps, but it was also exhilarating. My heart had pumped a little faster than usual. I was happy and relieved as we crossed the Channel homeward bound. I cast a last look at the French coast before it disappeared beneath the overcast of rapidly forming low stratus. The first mission and introductory operational sortie over enemy territory had gone well. Some pilots only ever made one trip. The shooting war had started for me and by early May I had completed a number of these armed excursions into northern France. It was to be a life of high adventure and thrills. Being a fighter-bomber pilot on the run up to D-Day, a year hence, one experienced days of dares, tensions, joys and fears, some anticipated, some totally unexpected. But it was a way of life for which I had been trained and one full of the intensities and excitement I had waited for. It would be hard to match anywhere.

My log book entry for 17 May 1943 reads: 'Ramrod 1.30 mins good bombing, lots of flak – jumped by enemy aircraft – quite an experience – 17 aircraft returned.' Let me expand. It was an early evening in the middle of May and two squadrons of Typhoons had taken off, each fully loaded with two 250-lb bombs and four 20 mm cannons; the target was Poix airfield some thirty miles inside France.

We formed up in a wing in squadron formation, three sections of three in each squadron, after completing one orbit over Tangmere below a height of 200 feet, necessary to avoid detection by the enemy coast radar units. The wing set heading for the French coast, and flew at roof-top level and below on occasions. I remember looking up at the chimney tops as we coasted out somewhere near Brighton, and dived to sea level in loose battle formation. We maintained that formation and R/T silence until 15 miles from the coast, whereupon we closed up quickly and commenced climbing at maximum rate to cross the coast at minimum height of 8,000 feet, to enable us to avoid most of the light flak.

Soon we were running up to Poix airfield through lumps of heavy flak. In our bombing formation I was number three of the outside flight in echelon starboard of the second squadron, and therefore last to attack. The ground beneath became obscured by smoke from the bombs exploding ahead of me. I dive-bombed in the standard procedure, turned on my back and dived at an angle of about 60 degrees, appreciably steep from the pilot seat. On the way down there was lots of light flak, as if I was flying through light snow. Swirling from varying directions came glinting tracer bullets twisting and winding their way up towards me through the evening darkness, bombs bursting and flashing on the cratered airfield below from the attacking aircraft ahead. It was an extraordinary awesome sight in the fading light. I released my bombs at about 2,000 ft and fired the four 20 mm cannons simultaneously, in a long ten second burst, strafing the dispersed parked aircraft on the ground. Then I pulled out at low level over the target area, quickly breaking off and away, banking left and pulling up to reform in squadron with all possible speed.

I had just rejoined when the number three (I recognized his voice) of the starboard section reported enemy aircraft at nine o'clock above, attacking. I looked up and saw four Messerschmitt 109s, 2,000 ft above, descending to attack. Being number three and last in the port section heading west, I was the nearest aircraft to the enemy fighters.

That was when complications arose, entirely of my own making. I had decided that for no other reason than sheer curiosity that on this occasion, one of my earliest operational sorties, I must see the black cross of a German aircraft at close quarters. So I kept my head turned and watched closely as these four yellow-nosed ME 109s descended on me like a swarm of wasps and attacked from the port rear. I did just glimpse the black cross of the leader as they closed down on me and was satisfied. I then turned around to find, surprisingly, the squadron had disappeared from sight while enemy bullets were flashing past and around me. My reflex action was to start an aileron turn and dive at great haste for the ground, streaking for the anonymity of cloud and haze cover some 8,000 ft below. Fortunately the haze layer was reasonably thick, from below about 4,000 ft, which afforded me some protection from those on my tail. Features below were difficult to distinguish except for the River Somme, which was over to my left.

I was now at full bore at 400 mph and right on the deck, and there I remained all the way over and out of France. I remember at one stage flying low in a valley looking up at a sloping village main street. I saw a Frenchman and two girls walking arm in arm, wave down to me and all gave me the vigorous V-sign as I flashed by below them. I returned the salute energetically. I kept glancing back to see if the 109s had gone, but they were still there on my tail, two on either side just discernible in the haze. My only chance of escape was to keep really low, hedgehopping to the English Channel over anything that would give me cover like buildings and trees, and fly deep in the valleys while peering ahead for the coastline.

After what seemed an incredibly long time I reached the French coast and nipped a few feet down to sea level, but had only gone about 400 yds out when there was a terrific resounding bang from the engine and streams of black smoke poured from either side. I felt a chill of disquiet as the engine cut. A dramatic silence prevailed. In all the excitement of the past hour I had committed the grave error of forgetting to change fuel tanks at the predetermined time. It was either intuition, or just good luck that as the bang occurred I automatically and instantly switched fuel tanks, and simultaneously pulled up from sea level. I had reached about 800 ft, was fast losing momentum at near stalling speed, and ready to bale out, when the engine surged back into life. I recall no panic, accepting that it just happened.

There was no sign of the four 109s as I looked around. Somehow they had lost me in the haze, most fortunately for me as I would surely have been killed had they seen me then, but there was still an awful lot of sea to cross. It was now getting dark. Alone above the water I switched on my navigation lights. I flew low and fast in a north-westerly direction and after what seemed ages, just when I was beginning to feel uncertain of my position and thinking of calling for help, with great relief I sighted the English coast in the distance. It turned out to be the distinctive promontory of Selsey Bill, my favourite marker during operations at Tangmere. So I wasn't too far off track after all. I felt safe and all anxiety disappeared.

I landed at Tangmere in the dark about a quarter of an hour behind the squadron, excited, profoundly shaken and short of fuel. As I climbed out and jumped to the ground I was surprised to find my hand shaking slightly and my mouth a little dry. The communique and station statistics that day could quite easily have read 'sixteen aircraft returned', with two of our aircraft missing. The one pilot lost came from the other squadron.

A normal Typhoon fighter-bomber mission was a concerted heavy single- or two-pronged attack of a fairly standard pattern. The target or targets for the day and sometimes the following day would come through to the squadrons from the higher echelon of operational Headquarters, at Group or Command. Timing of the attack would be agreed at 'wing' level and a meteorological followed by a *modus operandi* briefing held at one of the squadron dispersals about an hour before take-off. That gave sufficient time for everyone to get back to dispersal, don flying kit and prepare and discuss last minute tactical details within the squadron.

The number of aircraft involved together with the pilots selected for the mission had already been established, the total number for the 'wing' being a maximum of twenty-four aircraft, twelve in each squadron. There were circumstances when one squadron would borrow an aircraft from the other. Flying so much together the interdependence of the squadrons in all aspects was automatic. Those New Zealand guys were great friends, easy to fly with, and pleasant to talk to. We made a good team.

Ten minutes before scheduled take-off time, all pilots would stroll to their aircraft, strap themselves into the cockpit

The 'Wing' at Tangmere 1943–4. No. 197 and No. 486 NZ Squadrons

and await the wing leader to start his engine. On the signal twenty-four Sabre engines would fire, the bang from the cartridges resounding across and shattering the early morning stillness of the aerodrome. Hoods would be closed, faces would then quickly disappear beneath helmets, oxygen masks and goggles if used. I never used mine as they restricted vision. Only occasionally did we leave an aircraft behind unable to start. Experience by then had taught the right blend of treatment between cartridge starter, Kigas primer and engine temperature.

The noise level of the wing of Typhoons starting up and taxiing out for take-off was impressive, and the roar of the mighty Sabre as it became airborne conveyed power and confidence to all concerned. Those not on the mission were all out to watch the formidable power of the twenty-four pilots, 50,000 hp, ninety-six 20-mm cannon and forty-eight 500-lb bombs taking to the air. Once airborne and away we left behind a silent aerodrome; somethng I seldom experienced.

The take-off procedure was always the same. The aircraft from the lead squadron would line up on the runway and at the precise scheduled moment, the wing leader, using a stop-watch, would signal his moving and, releasing brakes, roll with his number two; each pair then followed closely in turn. The second squadron would repeat the procedure and take off as quickly as possible to ensure a speedy join up. In the meantime the wing leader remained low, flying relatively slowly on a wide circuit of the aerodrome. Each following pair cut corners to join up rapidly in formation in their respective positions.

Within one complete circuit of the aerodrome the wing was formed up in tight formation, wing tips overlapping and only a few feet apart. It was something of an ordeal to hold position while turning in a mass of aircraft at very low altitude at low speed and fully loaded. The rear enders had to cope with the turbulent slipstream effects of the planes ahead and there was an excessive use of the throttle as each pilot in turn was continually adjusting power settings. The concentration was enormous, sweat pouring out of everyone aboard. In the hot summer months we could feel the perspiration running in streams down the middle of the back and inside each leg of our flying suit. We were soaked before setting heading for France.

Once that ordeal was over and we had straightened out on an initial heading, the formation loosened and flying became much easier. Spread out, semi-relaxed, it could be pleasant as we sped across the Channel at about 200 ft and 300 mph. There was always the element of danger if the engine didn't behave itself. Bad weather conditions could cause some anxiety but generally low level crossings gave little cause for concern. Some pilots complained of that damned water continually below us and saw the land with gratitude, albeit the enemy's.

We then moved southwards in absolute radio silence, until in the distance a dark blue shrouded line ahead indicated the French coast. Within 15 miles of the coast squadrons commenced climbing, rapidly tightening up formation, aiming to cross inbound at about 8,000 ft to take us above the concentrated light flak belt that was encountered on every trip.

The spare aircraft, 'arse end charlie', not always available, would then return to base if no other aircraft had already precipitately done so; if so he took his place in formation. A precise navigation check was made as we crossed the coast and an alteration of heading to make our target area was completed if necessary.

We climbed steadily to optimum diving altitude. This could vary between 12,000 and 20,000 ft subject to prevailing meteorological conditions. Occasionally an aircraft fell away from the formation through lack of oxygen. One wing leader we had for a short time used the weather factor more than most by flying into and through the clouds using them as a cover. Many of us didn't appreciate his habit of being swallowed up in cloud, as our instrument flying (particularly *en masse*) was not all that proficient in those days. We sighed with relief after a few minutes as we broke into bright sunlight. We would rather have taken our chance with enemy fighters.

When at recommended bombing level and running up to target, radio silence was broken with the command 'bombs live'. At that we threw a switch. It was followed by another command to alter formation to echelon port or starboard position for the dive. That would depend either on previous information obtained from intelligence sources, on past experiences over target to avoid the worst anti-aircraft fire, or on the prevailing weather situation. It was here, directly over target, that we invariably encountered the heaviest concentration of both light and heavy flak. Sometimes a huge red marker would burst some miles ahead of us as the gunners below attempted to decipher our altitude. That red ball of fire looked more menacing than the clumps of black bursts that came later but we flew on regardless knowing well what was in store for us in the next few minutes. In early days it had been customary to weave a little to try and avoid most of the anti-aircraft artillery but sometimes one would fly into it instead of away from it. So we altered our tactics. We pressed on regardless, straight and level through the black horror hoping for the best. So we continued, listening to the well-directed heavy 'woof woof' of the forty- and eighty-eight millimetre shells exploding as they got too close for comfort.

Accurate navigation and quick location of the highly camouflaged targets was essential if we were to get out without undue loss and delay. It was always a relief when the first aircraft dived; we knew it would soon be over for yet another time, subject to the anticipated bit of luck. We never dwelt upon or worried about who was at the other end.

The high speed dive itself, usually out of the sun, was an impressive and thrilling experience, if it hadn't been so dangerous at times. Peeling off in turn, with an eye on the target, the aircraft was tilted and pulled up slightly above the horizon, then turned on to its back. The nose of the aircraft was then pulled down through the horizon, still turning and changing the direction of the turn, then straightening out to set up an angle of dive of about 60 to 70 degrees. This looked very steep indeed from the pilot's angle, appearing more like a vertical dive initially. The dive would continue at ever increasing speed, the nose of the aircraft aimed directly at the target below. The ground was now approaching so fast we had to avoid the danger and temptation of fixation of target and committing ourselves into a kamikaze attack by flying headlong into the target area. New pilots were warned of this dangerous phenomenon but now and again someone managed it.

Usually bombs were released at between 3,000 and 2,000 ft. This enabled a pull out to be completed by at least 1,000 ft, leaving sufficient height to clear any hazards or high ground in the area. We climbed away rapidly avoiding the lower level cone of intense flak in which evasive action was useless. Sometimes we remained low purposely, continuing the dive at high speeds of 450 to 500 mph, flying to a shallow angle as we progressively got lower to ensure the use of our four 20 mm cannons at a nearby alternative target.

Normally, however, immediately a dive-bombing attack was complete and bombs gone, each aircraft pulled sharply upwards, still pursued by flak. We usually turned left to reform in squadron loose formation away from the target area. Some pilots almost blacked out as they pulled out of the dive. The centrifugal force pressed one hard down into the seat: we all had to be careful of that. Some never came out of the dive and added to the fireworks below. It was an uncanny divorced feeling to sit and watch from height the activity of the others still involved in the fracas below, sitting waiting for the count when the attack was over, looking at the letters of each aircraft rejoining to find out who had 'bought it'. Up to three aircraft would be missing. Sometimes thankfully we were all aboard as we set heading for home.

Should there be a day when there was no specific bombing target allocated to the squadron we would proceed on one of three sweeps around the 'bus route'. The intention was to generate traffic in the form of enemy fighters or make strafing attacks on ground targets on an opportunity basis as they presented themselves. The adage 'Beware of the Hun in the Sun' was still operative but we never did see much of the 'Hun in the Sun' as air superiority had already been established by the Allies. There were a limited number of incidents with ME 109s and FW 190s which made our sorties productive.

The meeting with enemy or with friendly fighters, plus American long range (P51s) Mustang aircraft and crippled (B17s) Flying Fortresses returning from deep penetration daylight raids, filled the sky with aircraft. We rendezvoused and formed up with the friendly fighters under the code name

'Circus', and would then proceed to sweep an area *en masse*, covering a large part of the sky. That was known as a 'Balbo' sweep, the name derived from an Italian air ace of the past.

On the first bus route we crossed inbound north of Caen and flew on a large left-hand orbit taking Thury Harcourt, Falaise, Lisieux, Bernay, Rouen and Le Havre. We attacked targets at will, never returning without using all our ammunition. The second route saw us coasting in at Fécamp and overflying Serqueaux and Poix airfield, keeping our eyes peeled for enemy fighters taking-off below and searching every corner of the sky for small dots on the horizon. We strained our eyes up and into the sun hoping not to find them already lying up there in wait. We would then continue along the Somme and exit at Le Treport. The third bus route took us in the opposite direction, this time entering France at Bayeux, proceeding right to St Lo then on to Lessay and Cherbourg, coasting out at C'De La Hague. The targets here were camouflaged radio and radar installations, each heavily defended, and some shipping on the Cherbourg peninsula.

These missions were carried out in complete radio silence, paramount for safety reasons and only broken when absolutely necessary. We flew forever vigilant, keeping a sharp look-out but close enough to mime messages of action with our hands. All these sorties were invaluable experience and I was soon piling up operational hours, my aim for so long.

It was pleasant to walk across the airfield glistening with early morning dew in the spring, but this morning was dull, dark and dreary with mist and low cloud. I lifted my face to the coldness. It had started to rain, a soft fine rain. All was still and quiet in the grey gloom as I made my way to dispersal.

I was on the dawn cockpit readiness stint, two hours in flying kit, helmet on, harnessed to my Typhoon. Grabbing my flying gear I went up to the aircraft, strapped in and started the engine to warm it up, stopping it after a few minutes running. The time passed and I was just becoming uncomfortable sitting on the hard dinghy when the red Very light was fired from the control tower. The two of us were scrambled a few minutes before the relief was due. The Sabre engine roared with a bang as I pressed the cartridge start button. Quickly checking all instruments were functioning we took off straight across the airfield towards the control tower. Urgently bending the throttle fully open, quickly gathering speed, I careered ahead. Dropping optimum flap to shorten the take-off run, turning steeply left off the ground in my usual fashion, short of flying speed and sinking a little, I turned slightly, just missing the tower, on to a southerly heading. I urged the aircraft to go faster. It was chancy to fly in this manner but speed was essential and I knew my aircraft. I flew with experience, dash or by the seat of my pants as was my wont at the time. No thoughts of potential danger entered my mind. Assuming the aircraft was OK, I knew all would be well.

Retracting wheels and flaps, switching to approach control for an initial steer the second I was airborne, I remained at roof-top level picking up speed very quickly and had crossed the coast within thirty seconds, travelling low and fast over the sea, speed near 400 mph. I searched intently across the dull restricted horizon. Even with the poor visibility and low cloud that shrouded the Channel, the enemy aircraft, an ME 109 was sighted quickly directly ahead of us, a sitting duck heading back towards France, his dirty deed completed. I called my number two and said sharply over the radio:

'Enemy aircraft ahead, twelve o'clock, closing fast.' Checking guns and gunsight, turning gun button to fire, I closed on him much too fast and was forced to throttle back, drop some flap and turn right to avoid overshooting, so as not to become his target. My number two, Wally Ahrens, found himself in the same predicament, and as I banked right he went left. Even this action was barely sufficient to keep us behind the enemy aircraft. We came up on either side of this light green, yellow-nosed ME 109, flying line abreast with wing tips almost touching. I found myself staring at the black cross outlined in white on the fuselage. I saw the pilot's face staring at me, eyes wide with horror, then looking at Wally, then switching back to me like an animal at bay. He hadn't seen us until that moment. I could see the whites of his eyes. Our adversary was nervous, his face looked small, white and frightened and he didn't attempt to escape. He must have felt helpless with one great Typhoon either side of him, breathing down his neck.

This was the first German aircraft I had seen at *very* close range. It was fascinating, and it was almost its downfall. Reacting quicker than our foe, both of us slipped smartly behind him as we rapidly slowed down. The ME 109 large in

In my favourite aircraft, OV–X, shooting at an ME 109. This is a fine painting presented to me by E.H. Day in 1973, thirty years after the action

Wally Ahrens, killed in action (Imperial War Museum)

my gunsight filled my windscreen, and without more ado we instantly fired a long burst from our four 20 mm cannons, Wally firing first to great effect. His cannon fire raked the wings and engine of the Messerschmitt. As the shells hit the engine a streak of red flame spurted back towards me and black oil sprayed over the ME 109's wings. The pilot's perspex hood flew off backwards and shattered into fragments glinting and scattering in all directions. But we lost the 109 as he suddenly popped into the base of the low cloud. Hurt maybe, but he was one that got away, much to our disgust. It was with mixed feelings that I cruised back to base.

To me then, another day of the war had just begun. I landed thirty minutes after take-off, was released from readiness, and after interrogation and debriefing proceeded to breakfast and a hot bath.

Wally Ahrens, a tall Canadian with a habitual solemn expression interrupted occasionally by an enigmatic smile, was later promoted to squadron leader and was posted to another

squadron, only to be killed in action some months later. He
baled out on a low level bombing mission after being hit by
flak, but his parachute failed to open before he hit the ground.

It became apparent from intelligence reports later in the day
that low-flying enemy intruder aircraft had attacked military
targets on the Isle of Wight where two airwomen had been
killed. Our Messerschmitt 109 had been one of these aircraft.
Other aircraft were caught under similar circumstances later
that day and at least two enemy raiders were destroyed before
reaching the haven of the French coast. The target on the Isle of
Wight had been a ground control interception (GCI) station.
That equipment, when working in sychronization with a plan
position indicator (PPI) and other GCI stations along the south
coast, gave range and bearing information of enemy intruder
aircraft, and enabled the air traffic controller to indicate a
convenient interception heading for defending aircraft to steer.
The mission completed that morning was a good example of
how well the system worked.

A similar incident happened when two of us, sitting in our
Typhoons, were positioned at immediate readiness on the cliff
tops near Beachy Head. Many intruders on sneak sporadic hit-
and-run raids, usually ME 109s and or FW 190s, had been
attacking the towns of Brighton, Eastbourne, Hastings and
others in the area. Our base was too far away to be functional
against these attacks, so temporary landing strips of
Sommerfeld matting, named after the inventor, were laid on the
cliff tops. They were short, but adequate for precautionary
landings and emergency take-offs. The idea was to sit there all
day if necessary and await developments. The sweltering heat
in the hot cockpit from the high summer sun was a
considerable discomfort, but when scrambled to chase and
destroy the intruders it was made worthwhile.

I had been sitting in the open cockpit most of the morning,
looking at the shimmering sea and thinking a variety of

thoughts, when the ground field radio telephone went. We were informed that two lots of hit-and-run raiders were attacking targets locally. We scrambled immediately, holding on the brakes until almost full power for a short emergency take-off run, avoiding the birds which rose directly ahead, only the odd one exploding on the leading edge of the wings. Dipping low over the sea we set heading as directed by Air Traffic Approach Control, and gave chase to intercept the raiders. The enemy aircraft were sighted nearly halfway across the Channel. We came up fast from behind and I engaged one of them in combat. Having seen me he decided to turn steeply to the left, right on the deck, his wing tips almost touching the waves. Instinctively I kicked into a maximum power steep turn and settled in behind him. Putting down a little flap, to tighten the turn and lower my stalling speed, I tried to get sufficient deflection to open fire but it was difficult and highly dangerous at this low level. I noticed out of the corner of my eye the white breakers on the turbulent sea skimming my port wing tips. The menace was distracting.

The perfect killing deflection shot never materialized. Being unable to fire I waited behind, following tightly in ever decreasing circles, knowing what was likely to happen. We had gone through 360 degrees twice, tightening up the turns continuously, at a speed of about 250 to 300 mph. Glancing at the enemy, the airspeed and the cruel sea in turn with the engines roaring at full power, it was imperative I didn't cross controls and slip into the sea. In some cases pilots entirely forgot the altitude of the aircraft when concentrating only on keeping sights on the enemy. We were now almost vertical, standing on wingtips, and it was difficult to hold. I blinked the sweat out of my eyes. God, it looks a bit dangerous, I thought – when the FW 190, the arch rival of Typhoons, suddenly flicked twice in the opposite direction, crashed and sank like a stone into the sea, rapidly disappearing. The pilot of the FW 190 had tightened up his turn so much that he had manipulated his aircraft into a high speed stall, with a resultant flick in the opposite direction and complete loss of control. The Typhoon could just out-speed (and speed was often the difference between life and death), out-turn and out-manoeuvre the FW 190. With my superior speed and fighting power I kept the pressure on him so that what eventually happened was almost inevitable. That little amount of flap I used made my stalling speed that much lower, so I had felt relatively safe. Should action have taken place at a higher level the result and tactics could have been different, but in that situation the enemy aircraft would have had nowhere to go except up, and I would surely have had him anyway.

In the meantime my number two, Tanner Coles, had chased the other FW 190 who had refused to do battle all the way back to the French coast, and returned to join me as I waited for him. We returned low over the sea to our permanent base at Tangmere. Two other aircraft had been dispatched to take over at Beachy Head for the remainder of daylight. It is sad to report that Tanner Coles, a smiling and quietly optimistic Englishman who concealed a taste for adventure, was destined to be killed in a minesweeper roadstead operation some months later. He was hit by flak from the ships but it wasn't until the attack was over and we had climbed to height on our way home that Tanner's aircraft was seen to be in trouble.

I left formation and flew alongside him, signalling and calling on the R/T to try and attract his attention but he didn't stir. He was slumped in his seat, head lolling to one side and unable to answer or use his radio. I gave a parting salute he did not see. It was unusual to witness such a shallow glide. The aircraft was almost perfectly trimmed and travelled with wings level for miles over the sea, streaming glycol and white smoke until he finally hit the water. We watched him die unable to help. Earlier, three aircraft had been lost in the sea on a similar mission from the New Zealand Squadron that accompanied us. I witnessed all three of them descending into the deep to join so many others down there, hundreds, perhaps thousands, who had perished before them.

It's hard for most of us to appreciate what it must be like going into aerial combat, but if you've done it then you don't ever forget it. The adrenalin flows and you don't think too much about the danger to your own life. You are in there to win, and you do your best to shoot the other guy down. If you do you don't feel too desperate about it, because that's what you were there to do in the first place. If you hadn't got him he could have got you. You are keyed up all the time, there is no doubt about that, and when you land and it's all over there is a feeling of exhilaration about what you have accomplished.

Some days later Wing Headquarters sanctioned an operational fighter sweep. It certainly alleviated our boredom at dispersal which was near its peak as the bad weather kept us idle. The sweep was to differ from routine strafing and dive-bombing. It was a beautiful afternoon. The sky was cloudless, the sun bright. Only slight haze covered the English channel as we coasted outbound over the smooth waters of the Solent. Two squadrons of Typhoons accompanied by two Spitfire squadrons headed for France, to sweep the area of Bernay, Beaumont and Tricqueville. Our aim was to tempt FW 190s and ME 109s into the air: we were looking for trouble. Coasting inbound we circled one way, then the other on an ever widening arc, to no avail. All enemy aircraft remained firmly on the ground. Only sporadic flak from Lisieux interrupted our uneventful journey.

With a sense of disappointment we turned for home. As I looked down the French coast lingered under my starboard wing then slipped away as we headed north. Only the hazy horizon of the channel was visible. Through the steady drone of my Sabre engine came the loud and clear voice of

Tangmere's air traffic controller: would we divert and try to find the crew of a (B17) Flying Fortress, which had ditched in the sea to the west of us? It had been returning from a daylight bombing raid on the Ruhr. The crew were thought to have baled out.

Turning west in wing formation we headed into a golden haze of the sinking sun and the sea. We faced a pin-pointing problem. We had to spread into battle formation and cover a large area of the Channel. During that eye-straining exercise someone turned his head and looked down sun. He espied the tiny dot of a yellow dinghy in the drifting sea mist below. The Spitfires descended to give low level cover by orbiting over a wide area while in our Typhoons we remained at height. We patrolled between the French coast and the survivors until air sea rescue teams reached them. They were all rescued before nightfall. We turned and set heading for base. Our journey had been worthwhile after all. One of our aircraft crash-landed at Tangmere.

In June the squadron left on temporary detachment for a three week air-to-air gunnery course shooting at drogues at Martlesham Heath, Suffolk, and then returned to a spate of scrambles at Tangmere. Sitting in the cockpit we could now be airborne within fifteen seconds.

July 1943 to January 1944 were bad months for our squadron with a major loss of pilots and planes, including two new squadron commanders. The first of the squadron leaders arrived one day and it seemed he was gone the next. We barely got to know his name. He was fitted out with a complete new flying kit, helmet, goggles, overalls and flying boots, and was also allocated a brand new Typhoon, recently painted with squadron identification letters.

It was his first and only operational journey with us. Our mission was a relatively deep fighter sweep penetrating further inland than normal, skirting around the far side of Paris, attacking any suitable target, air or ground. For this purpose we carried one long range fuel tank slung underneath one wing and a 250 lb bomb under the other, plus our normal armament of four 20 mm cannons.

The squadron leader gave the briefing, and as there were no questions we proceeded to the aircraft to meet take-off time. Awaiting his signal we started the engines, the noise of the aircraft filling the morning air as twelve Typhoons taxied out to the runway. We lined up on the runway as a squadron and took off rapidly in pairs, forming up in line astern in tight formation at low level as quickly as possible and set a direct heading for Paris. Easing the formation over the sea we continued in radio silence. Ten miles from the grey line of the French coast we started the climb, as normal, to cross inbound above the light flak belt. The weather over England had been clear when we departed, but as we passed over France at 10,000 ft, large amounts of broken strato-cumulus clouds were quickly developing. They built up more and more as we reached the Paris area.

Dodging the billowing cumulus cloud tops we flew above in brilliant blue sky, the wide expanse of a clear-cut horizon broken only with sporadic bursting balls of black heavy flak penetrating through the clouds. We continued en route. The flak increased as we swung left far to the south of Paris. We went further than intended, and it was with growing apprehension I watched my fuel gauges ebb as we continued round in a wide sweep on to a reciprocal heading, homeward bound.

I was flying in open battle formation, number two to the new squadron commander when suddenly his aircraft was badly hit. He quickly lost height, leaving a thick heavy trail of dark smoke behind him. I left the squadron, eased the throttle back and began to close in from battle formation towards him. I followed him down in a descending turn to the left, hoping I could see what was wrong and maybe get a signal from him, as he seemed unable to use the radio. I closed in more tightly and held station as we neared the cloud tops but was unable to help in any way. I waved goodbye, but I don't think he saw me, being busy inside the cockpit. As he penetrated the clouds and disappeared I pulled hard left, and climbed up full throttle to rejoin the squadron some 10,000 ft above, positioning myself as arse-end Charlie above and behind, weaving about to keep a good look-out for enemy fighters. On the return leg we bombed a target north of Dieppe and there lost another aircraft, which finally crashed into the sea. We assumed both the aircraft and pilot had been hit by light flak which had entered through the large radiator into the glycol tank. The loss of that caused rapid seizure of the engine. The pilot was killed as the aircraft exploded on hitting the water, where it was quickly swallowed up.

Before reaching base, yet another pilot made a surprisingly dramatic exit and ejected. He fell from the belly of the aircraft as he turned it upside down just off the white cliffs at Beachy Head. He was about 1,000 ft up in the sky, at the end of his parachute. I watched him drift gently to earth. It took him only a few minutes. Baling out was preferable to ditching. We were all aware that a Typhoon ditching was at its best an unenviable experience, in all probability fatal, particularly if it was into a rough sea during winter months.

Another aircraft then crash landed at base; the pilot was unhurt. So ended the mission. Our squadron was relatively new and, except for a few of us, still operationally inexperienced. Therefore it was upsetting on our return to count the damage for what was quite an ordinary trip. It had been a memorable but unfortunately disastrous mission, with the loss of four aircraft and two pilots. The pilot who baled out was fortunate enough to land at low tide, and was picked up later, but for one squadron on one sortie it was a heavy penalty.

We carried on in this vein with missions increasing in tempo throughout the remainder of 1943 and 1944, attacking a multitude of targets. Radar sites, railway yards, radio installations, receiver masts, airfields, trains, staff cars, water towers, minesweepers, columns of infantry and any other installations of military significance were at the mercy of the Typhoon. Between Dunkirk and Brest there were at least sixty radar installations, all priority objectives, all heavily defended; to attack them continually and survive demanded skill and daring together with a bit of luck. Systematic destruction of those radar units was an essential prerequisite for the intended invasion.

Losses of aircraft and experienced pilots was heavy on all squadrons. It caused a dearth of Typhoon pilots, but the replacements filling those slots were arriving on the squadrons with less than ten hours on type, some as low as five. I felt sorry for these newcomers to the wing. Their operational training had been severely curtailed, so they could barely fly the aircraft with any confidence, let alone fly one that was fully loaded into a tight, low level and rapidly forming, hot, sticky and turbulent wing formation. It was extremely difficult for them and formations looked a bit ragged at times. There were brief moments that were highly dangerous immediately after take-off due to these uncertainties and inexperience. I felt some of those pilots would have been better suited to another command.

By this time, with an immense amount of luck; I had accrued more than 200 hours on Typhoons, some of them at night. It was a good deal more than most, for obvious reasons. With that experience I had achieved status and was now a permanent section leader. I felt full of inner confidence. Maybe I was overconfident because we few hardened veterans considered ourselves to be invincible, with a tenacious hold on immortality. We believed in the philosophy that danger was inversely proportional to the number of missions completed; so we kept asking for more. We seemed indestructible, and felt more so the longer we survived

Our operational sorties had a variety of different code names. They were against targets of specific military or strategic importance and could be a Roadstead, a Rhubarb, a Ramrod, a Ranger or a Recce, as allocated by Group Headquarters. A Roadstead was a low level attack against shipping; a Rhubarb was a low level attack on specific targets, when the weather conditions were such that dive-bombing was impossible; a ramrod was a high level bombing attack on selected targets. Taking risks galore I completed nearly a hundred of those without so much as a scratch, but could easily enough have been lost on any one of them. A Ranger was an extra long sortie, when one carried additional fuel tanks and penetrated further inland looking for enemy aircraft or suitably vulnerable ground targets. The ancillary fuel tanks were used first and ejected when empty, or immediately if combat was inevitable. A Recce was a similar exercise without the extra fuel, like a sweep of the normal bus route. One or more of these sorties was carried out on a daily basis by either the wing, squadrons, flight, four or just two aircraft, weather permitting.

Today it was a Ramrod and again I was flying number two (because of my experience, and ready to step to the front if required) to another new squadron commander, who had been

'Jacko' Holmes in front of his Typhoon (OV-2) with his small dog (Imperial War Museum)

with us a relatively short time. The target was a V1 site some thirty miles inland near Abbeville. We expected a straightforward dive-bombing operation with no complications. We taxied out in exemplary order and took off in pairs as scheduled on the shimmering runway. It was a clear day and a pleasant enough journey flying low over the smooth shining waters of the Channel. Climbing before the French coast, and holding radio silence, we changed formation to echelon starboard position for the dive. It had been done so often it was now simply routine.

Our new commanding officer was a dark curly-haired, rotund and happy man with a loud infectious laugh. He was a

'Jacko' Holmes taxiing out before his fatal flight (Imperial War Museum)

fount of wit and wisdom, and full of charisma; we all liked him. 'Jacko' Holmes lived with enormous gusto, a volcano of energy. They killed him over Abbeville, blasting him out of the sky in a ball of red fire. They hit him as he was travelling at 400 mph, with a lucky shot from below.

He was first to start the dive with me following quickly behind. Staying close and slightly to one side I followed him down with the others diving closely behind in turn. 'Jacko' had only just got settled into his dive when his Typhoon stunningly exploded into a huge ball of brilliant red fire, the flames enveloping the whole of his aircraft. I was perilously near, only feet away to the right side and slightly behind when he blew up in my face. I heard the dull thud of the explosion over the noise of my roaring engine. I was momentarily numbed by the sight and surprised at the massive ball of fire as I screamed past him at 8,000 ft diving at nearly 500 mph and peering deep into the flames, looking for something solid that would give me hope that he was still alive. But the cone of fire was red throughout and there was no dark shape of an aircraft inside. He had carried a good luck talisman hung round his neck, but to no avail.

I continued down to target, the ack-ack still pounding away, released my bombs, then continued lower strafing, filled with righteous anger. The squadron followed my natural reactions using all their ammunition, and in turn pulled up to re-form behind me. I led the squadron home that day, unusual for a flight sergeant pilot. What should have been a proud and profoundly satisfying accolade was diminished by our tragic loss. Jacko's death was a stinging, sad blow to all of us. He had been a tremendous tonic to the squadron; his dynamic spirit and jolly manner had been infused into all the pilots, not only on our squadron but throughout the wing.

The Cherbourg peninsula targets were notorious for being most heavily defended. The thick flak was a deterrent and we were always apprehensive when a sortie was planned that took us over the Cherbourg area. A single massive crimson marker cloud staining the sky some miles ahead of the formation was an ominous indication of the trouble we were flying into. As the formation continued towards the target a tremendous barrage of bursting black puffs opened up immediately ahead of our flight level.

I was up in the earliest dawn groping for my clothes on a cold dark morning in January 1944 and quickly headed for the dispersal, being picked up by squadron jeep. An illegal light shone out from the guardroom as we drove past. This morning I was setting off ahead of the main stream of aircraft, acting as a pathfinder. It was the toughest, most exacting and responsible task assigned me to date, but I was proud to be entrusted with

and selected for the assignment. I was to fly ahead, locate and
mark the target to ensure that wing formation time over target
was cut to the minumum.

As I climbed into my aircraft there were signs of a new day
in the sky. The clouds were high and the sun was rising on the
horizon as I took off and kept very low, turning and heading in
a south-south-westerly direction. It was a long lonely haul of a
hundred miles across the Channel early that morning, but I kept
up a fast speed, acknowledging the odd ship by dipping one
wing as I sped by.

The target, photographs of which I had previously studied,
was well concealed by natural camouflage, positioned in a
wood some miles south of the town of Cherbourg. I was hoping
it could be easily and speedily identified. Visibility was good
as I climbed rapidly to altitude. The usual barrage of flak met
my arrival. Endeavouring to avoid it precluded any other
thoughts. As I continued south through the stuff towards the
hidden target, the flak intensity increased. Success in this
mission was imperative. The wing were relying on me to
pinpoint and visually mark the exact spot in order to make their
run direct and avoid time over the flak-ridden target area. I was
aware of this responsibility as heavy flak burst perilously close
and encircled me. I had to take further evasive action. With
heart thudding, circling, twisting and searching, time seemed
eternal but was probably only a few minutes; I was expecting
to be blasted to Kingdom Come at any moment.

Reading from a folded map strapped to my knee, with relief
I spotted the hutted encampment and the narrow road leading
to the pylon transmitter. That special combined radar
installation and radio beam transmitter, once used by the
German night firelighting pathfinder and bomber force
attacking England, was certainly beautifully camouflaged.
Quickly I rolled over, no fear or hesitation, and with cool
confidence started the bombing run. It had to be accurate. With

intense concentration I pressed on, lower and lower, regardless of the light flak, until I was certain I couldn't miss. Dropping both delay bombs, I continued low over the target firing all ammunition from the four cannons. Passing overhead with a speed of 450 mph I pulled up, banked to the left, and glimpsed with satisfaction the illuminated target through the smoke and fire. With adrenalin bubbling I dived low again and set heading for home. I flew low back over the Channel at high speed, tense with excitement but confident of the success of the mission. Wing attack was sure to go well. Suddenly I was aware of and worried about an unusual deep vibration sound from the rear of the aircraft. I must have been hit, I concluded. Nothing showed as I searched around the cockpit and looked outside over the wings and tailplane. The engine was thankfully running smoothly but I climbed a little higher. I reached base safely, flew over the control tower for a visual check, but no damage could be seen. I joined the circuit, landed, taxied safely into dispersal and switched off, uttering an exclamation of relief and pleasure.

Opening the cockpit canopy to let in the cool morning air, I noticed the flight commander, Rex Mulliner, with a cheerful grin on his face. As I jumped on the ground, I automatically turned and hit the metal disc to release my parachute, and he came forward as I started undoing my Mae West life jacket.

'How did it go?'

'Very well, fine, I think,' I replied. 'The target was a bit difficult to find being so small and heavily camouflaged. There was quite a lot of flak and I think I've been hit somewhere; there was some vibration and the aircraft was a bit troublesome on the low dash across the Channel – so I'm glad to be back.'

'Fine,' he acknowledged. 'In that case how would you like to lead a flight of four on a Rhubarb around the Abbeville area in about an hour's time? Group Headquarters have just come through with a possible target.'

I thought for a few moments before answering. Something was wrong. I didn't want to go. Succinctly I informed him of my refusal, emphasizing that I would be happy to go on anything that came up after lunch.

'Okay Jimmie,' he replied evenly. 'I'll get someone else.' I walked away. This was the first and only offer of an operational sortie I ever declined.

Rex finally selected a pilot called Miles, a quiet, dark, dimpled, pious Welshman, with an air of innocence. He was a devoted Christian, praying on his knees by his bedside every night. I remember we got him high on a couple of pints of cider one night. He limped home happily with one foot on the pavement and one in the gutter. He was slightly less experienced than myself but relatively more so than many others in the squadron. The mission went ahead as planned, but it was to be costly. Miles never came back, nor did two of the others. It seemed as if I'd had a premonition. My luck was still holding. We spent a sombre and silent evening when we heard the melancholy news and immense loss to the flight, the squadron and the unit.

The target for another day was a roadstead, against two 2,000 ton minesweepers operating at the mouth of the River Seine estuary, near Le Havre harbour. Two squadrons of Typhoons, fully armed with two 500 lb bombs and 20 mm cannons took off to sink them. Forming up as normal we set heading at low level for Le Havre. Some twenty minutes later, with the clearly defined coast on either side of us, twenty Typhoons headed down the estuary, all eyes searching the wide expanse of the river mouth for the minesweepers. We found them close together, further in towards Le Havre than anticipated, and I realized then there was going to be another hectic half hour ahead.

Keeping low, encircling the ships, we positioned ourselves for the run, ensuring the attack would be made away from land

and the shore batteries; allowing anyone hit to keep heading
north away from flak-infested France. It would help any pilot
to make his escape home, should ditching or parachuting be
necessary.

We made two attacks in pairs, dropping one bomb on each
attack and indulging in prolonged cannon fire the second time
round. On these low strafing attacks the long range of the 20
mm cannons was important and used to advantage. We used to
fire a quick burst at long range avoiding skid or side slip by
ensuring the turn and bank indicator was in the centre. The
results could be seen well ahead. It was then easy to adjust the
angle of the aircraft and correct the aim if necessary, and hit the
target with precision and a great deal of satisfaction. The
technique was employed with success on all targets, land and
sea.

The furious flak from both ships and shore batteries was
murderous. Only the north-west corner of the lower level
circuit gave us a breather. Contending with this prolonged area
of flak, flying in patches of poor visibility in a foray of twenty
Typhoons, was no easy task. It needed concentration and the
odd bit of luck. We spent twenty minutes at zero feet in this
hellish cross fire, streams of shells smashing into some aircraft.
There were spectacular hits on the ships, as we kept pumping
cannon shells into them. Great balls of flame shot up into the
air. As we departed both minesweepers were blazing wrecks
and no longer effective, but we too had our casualties. Three of
our aircraft were missing: all had gone into the muddy water of
the estuary. On landing at base other aircraft were found
riddled with bullet holes. It had been a sortie of above average
intensity.

Another sortie of equal ferocity was to take place soon after at

St Malo, an historic old walled town at the mouth of the River Rance, with an extensive harbour. Results were similar. These minesweeper attacks, carried out regularly, were classified as something special and losses were to be expected. Only the luck of the draw saved you. Two of our aircraft did not return from St Malo.

The large open front radiator which helped to make the Typhoon look fearsome on the ground, particularly when painted with white or yellow sharks' teeth and other personal designs, could be its Achilles' heel in the air. One bullet through the large open grill could pierce the engine, and cause its seizure very quickly through the loss of glycol. We were always wary of that happening during heavy concentrations of flak, for some of our losses on these intense raids were caused by this vulnerability. It was also a reason for some unexpected ditchings, due to the delayed action of a small leak on the relatively long haul back home across the Channel.

Early in 1944 I was good-heartedly nicknamed the Abbeville Kid by some of the squadron pilots. Having survived so long I was almost twenty-two by then, and one of the oldest members of the squadron, with an operational record enabling me as a flight sergeant to be an established section leader. It was not uncommon for an experienced NCO to lead less experienced officers into battle in the air. I also had an aircraft of my own. Lettered OV–X, it apparently didn't mark the spot for the masses of German gunners firing from below. I felt uneasy if my aircraft was unserviceable and had to use another, but I guess most of us were a little superstitious.

Abbeville is a small town lying some thirty miles inside France on the north side of the River Somme, a river of some repute from a previous catastrophe. The Abbeville Kid nickname originated from my many sorties over and around this landmark, with its large marshalling yards, small and well-camouflaged V1 launching sites, and nearby active fighter airfields, which attracted Typhoons like wasps to a nest. This section of northern France, with its variety of military targets, was heavily defended, and stretched all the way from the Pas de Calais to the Cherbourg peninsula, and beyond to Brest. The concentrated fire of the light and heavy flak from the ground batteries was frightening to behold. It was like flying through oncoming snow or patches of little black clouds. A physical sense of relief and well-being permeated us each time we came through the ordeal. However, not too many of us experienced that enlightened feeling too often. No sooner had some pilots arrived to replace those missing, than they themselves were missing. We became impersonal and unfeeling when these new pilots we barely knew did not return.

As D-Day drew nearer the tension mounted as softening up operations for 'Overlord' were about to begin. There was a tremendous flood of activity as the wide-scale air offensive continued unabated and increased in intensity. The frequency and ferocity of the attack, wreaking havoc on all types of communications, was essential to paralyse the close concentration of radio and radar installations, expertly camouflaged and concealed along the whole northern coastline of France.

These attacks by both Fighter and Bomber Commands of the Allies certainly softened up the defences and, one supposes, were very satisfactory to higher command, but they also had a detrimental effect on the nervous system of some fighter-bomber pilots. Most of these radio and radar sites were utterly destroyed before the great day of the invasion arrived. While accomplishment of these prime objectives was undoubtedly successful, it was also debatable whether the sharp increase in

Taking the strain in the months before D-Day, at Tangmere

mortality and overall losses of pilots and aircraft was justified. From the pilots' point of view, in light of the risks involved, the imbalance probably favoured some reduction or even curtailment of those types of semi-kamikaze low level and dive-bombing attacks.

Nevertheless, morale of the Typhoon squadrons remained fairly high in those momentous days in the run up to the invasion of Europe. During the evenings at spontaneous convivial gatherings in the messes or elsewhere, with or without a piano, the rendering of many wartime and other songs was heard throughout the neighbourhood as we relaxed from the tensions of the day. Gregarious, lively, given to wild enthusiasm, we ostentatiously drove the fully loaded squadron jeep on pub excursions into Chichester and spent many a glorious evening in the Dolphin, the Ship, the Unicorn or the Nag's Head. Sometimes we went only as far as the local Tangmere Arms. I guess we were considered somewhat eccentric. As the night progressed revelry continued; it was wonderful to feel irresponsibility creeping over me. The inbibing of many pints of black and tan cushioned and converted fears into convulsions of laughter, and we brushed danger cheerfully aside. No one knew nor cared which party might be his last – and we didn't give a damn. One song from the repertoire that was frequently heard in unison was the 'Airmen's Lament'. We sang the ballad with much feeling and vigour. The chorus was particularly appropriate, and the words went something like this:

> Oh, a young aviator lay dying,
> He'd cracked up his very last plane,
> When asked if he had any message,
> He mournfully sang this refrain.

> Take the cylinders out of my kidneys,
> The spark plug remove from my brain,
> From the small of my back take the crankshaft,
> And assemble the engine again.

> When the Court of Enquiry assembled,
> To find out the reason he died,
> T'was a flat spin that closely resembled,
> The maximum angle of glide.

> So stand by your glasses steady,
> Here's good luck to the man in the sky,
> Here's a toast to the dead already,
> Three cheers for the next man to die.

> Cast away from the land that bore us,
> Cast away from the land that we love,
> All the best have gone before us,
> Good luck to the next man to die.

So stand by your glasses make merry,
Here's good luck to the man in the sky,
Here's a toast to the dead already,
Three cheers for the next man to die.

The dispersal locker room was smelling musty, of stale cigarettes and sweaty flying gear, as I stepped inside early one muggy May morning. I had been detailed to deliver a new Typhoon to RAF Manston, Kent and return with another aircraft. The journey seemed quite straightforward and I was anxious to have it over with and get back to base. The flight was not uneventful.

The aircraft was fitted with only the local tower radio frequencies of both aerodromes. The weather was considered suitable, a gun-grey gloomy day, an adequate cloud base with maybe some light rain en route. In the dim early morning light I lowered myself into the cockpit and started up, checked all instruments and controls were functioning correctly, decided all was well and taxied out for take-off.

Once airborne the intention was to keep below cloud and fly direct to Manston by means of a low level pilot navigation map reading exercise. I set heading on that basis. Less than half-way there, visibility steadily worsened, and the cloud ceiling lowered to sit on the Hampshire and Surrey downs. How far eastward it stretched I could not tell. It was impossible to get through it visually and to climb ahead could have been fatal, as I had no navigational or approach control radio aids to call for assistance on the descent. Instrument flying on fighter aircraft in those days was almost unheard of. Only a few pilots were proficient in long periods of cloud flying, but I wasn't one of them. I can barely remember using the artificial horizon during the war but was later to qualify as an instrument rating examiner while a flying instructor and so eventually used the instrument to excess. The alternative was to return to base. Not likely. I turned to starboard away from the cloud-decked hills towards the coast, and took the long way round.

I glanced at my watch, had been airborne only twenty minutes and had plenty of fuel. So, heading to the coast in a descending turn, I pressed on resolutely and resigned myself to an anxious flight. I flew along the serrated Sussex-Kent coastline, my port wing hugging the broad sweep of the chalk-white cliffs, feeling more apprehensive as weather and visibility deteriorated further into a curtain of constant drizzle.

I knew that if I could just keep visual with my wing tip abreast the cliff, it would be only a matter of time before I reached Manston. Then more troubles developed. First the engine began to vibrate; a fluctuating oil pressure was indicated on the instruments. The weather became murky, rain obliterating forward visibility, and without warning I found myself amid the balloon barrage hanging over Dover Harbour. Down through the gloom I could see balloons moored at ground level but couldn't see any cables from those airborne. The balloons at Dover had already claimed lives and it was with that thought in mind and more than a little panic that I weaved my way through the barrage at 300 mph.

Turning right and left, on intuition, dodging unseen cables and praying I wouldn't wrap myself around one of them for the cold sea to swallow me up, I pressed on. It seemed like an eternity before I was clear of all hazards. Abreast Deal the weather was clear enough and Manston lay ahead. The engine was still giving cause for concern but had got no worse. I arrived at Manston cursing the met. man and those who had sent me on this foolish errand.

I remained at Manston for lunch, looked around the dispersals and talked to some of the pilots from the incumbent squadrons. Late that afternoon I returned to Tangmere with a replacement aircraft. The journey back was uneventful until I got within a few miles of base. The perverse weather had cleared. The cloud base had risen and visibility, even though poor underneath, was better except for patches of intermittent light rain. I wasn't expecting anything untoward when the gremlins struck again. Four miles from touchdown on a straight approach the engine cut, coughed, spluttered and picked up, then spluttered again, a plume of smoke being emitted from either side.

I was fairly high, so sticking the nose down to keep up the speed I headed straight for touchdown. Nursing the engine with primer and throttle I managed to smack the aircraft down on the end of the runway, hard and fast at 160 mph, peering through an oil-filmed perspex windscreen in the drizzle and gathering darkness. The engine spluttered and stopped dead at the far end of the runway. The light drizzle suddenly turned into a downpour as I waited for the ground crew to present themselves.

What should have been two pleasant and simple ferrying trips turned out to be a hairy experience. In contemplation at the end of the day I decided I would rather have taken my chances over France.

There were few non-operational flights at Tangmere other than air tests. I remember on one of these climbing to 30,000 ft with a slight cold. On landing, my ears were blocked and slightly painful. I had to get back into the cockpit immediately on doctor's orders and climb all the way back up again to an altitude just passing 20,000 ft, when my ears cleared. Then I had to make a very slow controlled descent. The only other spare flying was an odd moonlight trip for night flying experience and familiarity should the need arise operationally.

The serviceability of Typhoons still left a lot to be desired. The new Napier Sabre engine continued to have technical snags and

Relaxing between flak-
ridden sorties

it was creditable to the mechanics that on most occasions they
were able to supply the requisite number of aircraft when an
important mission was scheduled.

Technical hitches didn't make it any easier for the pilot on
operations. In the early days there was a continual worry of
imminent danger. We wondered if the engine would get you,
even if the enemy didn't. The long sea crossing over the
Channel at low level was no joke with a suspect engine and
inclement conditions heightened the tension. Some pilots
turned back at the French coast with a suspect engine, or so
they said. There was a tendency to suspect some of them being
guilty of lack of moral fibre ('LMF') but this was difficult to
prove. Then there were additional worries about survival on
ditching a Typhoon. So it was always a relief to coast inbound,
albeit over France. The reliability of Sabre engines improved
dramatically after its modifications had eliminated practically
all faults. Strangely enough, here is when the law of averages

operated favourably for me, for even though I flew my Typhoon fast and to its limits I had no engine trouble on a full tour of operations – a most significant factor.

We had one particular aircraft on the squadron that you could set your watch by. It had been used on operations but the pilots concerned had all turned back with engine trouble. Its unserviceability was a complete mystery. The engineering staff could find no fault, so we took it in turns to fly it around the circuit while they stood and watched. Exactly twenty minutes after take-off, the engine could be heard cutting and spluttering overhead. The engineers gave up and called in the experts, and the aircraft was finally returned to the makers for further investigation. It was said that some aircraft had as many modifications as there were days in the year.

Towards the end of one long and uneventful day hanging around the dispersal, dealing with mundane tasks and ready to leave for the mess and high tea, the action started. The red Very from the control tower was carried by a cold gusty wind that swept across the aerodrome towards dispersal. Suddenly two of us were scrambled. Flight Sergeant Barnard and myself dashed across the grass for our aircraft, jumped frantically into our cockpits at record speed and took off in a climbing turn southward. I was so keen to get airborne I didn't bother to strap up. Some of my urgency must have communicated itself to my number two, as he didn't bother either. With blue section airborne, I called the tower and changed over to approach. Over the R/T from Approach Control came the message that an American aircraft was in trouble, being attacked by enemy aircraft in the Bay of Biscay.

I kept climbing, turning on to a south-westerly heading. We reached 25,000 ft in marginal weather conditions. A deep

depression was centred to the south-west of Lands End. Anvils
of ominous large cumulo-nimbus clouds embedded in the
approaching warm and cold fronts showed menacingly ahead, a
portent of bad weather to come. Away to port there were
massive thunderstorms, their latent energy being released and
displayed in rapid flashes of streak lightning; there, too, was
the beginning of a rainbow. Holding a heading of 225 degrees
magnetic, we travelled 150 miles searching the skies. I spotted
an American (P38) Twin Boom Lockheed Lightning about
5,000 ft below heading north, a small black dot against the
massive white background. At the same time two enemy
aircraft were noted farther south high in the sky. I took a glance
at my altimeter. We were still at 25,000 ft. I called my number
two and reported positions of both aircraft, turning as I did so.
With another quick shufty at the enemy aircraft, we kept
turning, diving left to rendezvous, and gradually easing
ourselves into position, one on either side of the American. We
came up in line abreast, wagging our wings, and acknowledged
a hand signal. Opening up into battle formation, flying slightly
above, we kept a sharp look-out for enemy fighters.

Within a few minutes two enemy fighters attacked from
above and behind the towering clouds, into a gap of clear sky.
Waiting and biding our time, I watched them closely as they
swooped down from starboard. I called my number two and
together we broke hard left and turned to meet them head on.
Closing rapidly, at nearly 1,000 mph, all guns firing, they gave
way, missing us by a hair's breadth as they flashed by overhead
in the climb. They continued climbing fast, passing well behind
the American Lightning, zooming up and disappearing, never
to return. They must have been short of fuel or ammunition not
to try again.

We turned quickly and using full power rapidly reformed
either side of our American friend, resuming escort
protection back to Britain without further accident. We did

spy two very high-flying objects at about 40,000 feet, above the broken cirrus cloud, speeding fantastically in the opposite direction, leaving behind ruler-straight condensation trails across the azure blue sky. I imagined them to be the contemporary phenomenon known as Foo Fighters, later to become Unidentified Flying Objects or UFOs. There was no encounter.

Flying high, west of Selsey Bill, the outline of the south coast, the Solent, Southampton waters and the Isle of Wight were displayed like a dark map below. The American Lightning continued inland on a north-easterly heading as we waved goodbye and turned for Tangmere. A 'strawberry' in the form of a congratulatory signal arrived from USAF headquarters next day for services rendered. An American VIP had been aboard.

As we approached Tangmere in the descent, with dusk fast approaching and darkening the skies, I was bounced by an American aircraft, this time not as a friend. He came at me from the west out of the sinking red sun, attacking from above as I descended through 10,000 feet.

I took immediate avoiding action to counteract his quarter attack. Using lots of bottom rudder and stick hard back, I broke towards him with a sharp violent turn to the left, flicking into a half-roll that pulled the aircraft down in the dive upside down, then hard round into an upward spiral using full power. He slipped past as I rolled over and pulled hard over, and followed him down. The dogfight continued for a few moments until I could get near enough to indicate I was friendly. This type of incident transpired with a number of American red-nosed (P47s) Thunderbolts, their pilots mistaking the Typhoon for a Focke-Wulf 190. The Typhoon was later painted with black and white stripes underneath and the nose spinner white among other things, for ease of recognition. The American pilot apologized profusely to me by phone that evening.

It was dark when Flight Sergeant Barnard and I left dispersal that evening, having witnessed two sunsets, the red ball of the sun again sinking below the horizon of the trees as we landed. We found the aerodrome calm with that strange quiet, peculiar to active airfields after the noise and bustle of the normal working day, as we chatted and strolled back to the mess. Soon afterwards 'Barney' was shot down and killed over northern France. He was a keen pilot, liked the battle, but unfortunately never got to see the end of the war or even the invasion of Normandy, which I'm sure his undoubted jingoism would have eagerly appreciated.

CHAPTER 6

Towards D-Day and Beyond

In April 1944 the squadron moved from Tangmere to a
temporary advanced landing ground at Needs Ore Point, an
area near the Solent. Two large fields were combined and a
runway made out of pre-fabricated Sommerfeld steel tracking.
Its steel mesh plates and sheeting were laid on an uneven strip
of ground, whose ups and downs caused difficulties for the
Typhoons on take-off and landing.

The propellor of the Typhoon is large and with the aircraft
tail up on take-off had only a 9 in clearance from the runway
surface. On one occasion two aircraft were scrambled, and in
the rush to get airborne the leading aircraft's nose was pushed
too far forward as it hurtled down the runway. The inevitable
happened. The propeller dug into the steel tracking on one of
the bumps and the Typhoon somersaulted, cartwheeled and
crashed into a mass of large and small pieces, still careering
down the field. The second aircraft, taking off in close
formation was unable to avoid the debris and cannoned into the
fire and flying metal, smashing up and adding to the horrifying
sight. The two aircraft were totally destroyed and two more
pilots lost their lives. We stood aghast and speechless as we
surveyed the horrible scene. The temporary runway was
quickly cleared of strewn wreckage and two replacement
aircraft took off in a delayed answer to the scramble.

We were now four squadrons – 257, 266, 193 and ourselves,
197 – in 84 Group, Second Tactical Air Force, under 'canvas'
with a mobile tactical and intelligence headquarters. We
awaited further deployment with the oncoming of operation
'Overlord' and our subsequent Normandy-based activities.

Pseudo scout life under canvas was a startling overnight change from the warmth and comfort of our Tangmere abode. That rough and ready camp environment continued for the remainder of my tour with the squadron, some four months. It was comfortable enough, the food was good and there was a shower available somewhere in the field. I soon acclimatized.

Towards the end of May the wing set out on an armed Recce/Rhubarb from our temporary base. The weather was perfect with good visibility, and an adequate amount of broken strato-cumulus cloud giving necessary cover. We remained low over the Channel, climbing only to between 2,000 and 3,000 ft as we coasted inland. Cruising in open formation at 300 mph searching, finding, bombing and strafing all the military targets to be found. There were some juicy targets on offer.

We had one long range tank and one 500-lb bomb. These stores enabled us to penetrate that much further inland looking for individual targets. On previous raids I had hit many trains, tanks and other potentially explosive targets with impressive results, great balls of fire spurting skyward.

That particular armed Recce turned out to be a hectic two hours for most of us. A good deal of damage was done to a variety of targets. The total tally for the wing was impressive. Acting separately as squadrons, then flights subdividing into sections and pairs, we accounted for six ME 109s destroyed, three more 109s damaged and two probables, together with crippling strikes on bridges, trucks, staff cars, gun positions and other installations.

There had been little enemy aircraft opposition. The Luftwaffe by then was a spent force and almost inactive as we bombed and strafed at will. Flying at tree-top level, hedge-hopping, avoiding protruding hazards, we could have read the signposts had we slowed down. There had been some patchy defensive fire but the light flak had claimed no casualties. It was a good day for all concerned and there was much rejoicing and many tales to relate on return. Naturally we were jubilant at the results, particularly so as we had sustained no losses. Not one of our aircraft was missing.

Eager to swap experiences, the celebration started early that evening and later shook the rafters of the nearby hotel at Beaulieu as we gradually exaggerated our wild stories with appropriate hand actions. The party continued until the early hours of the morning back in our tented equipment. As the excitement wore off among those of us who remained, we found ourselves lulled to a sentimental lugubrious state as tiredness and the demon drink took its toll.

These nights of debauchery were easily forgotten as our exultant, youthful high spirits and ecstatic feelings for the world of operational flying took over early the next day.

Another day two squadrons took off from the advanced landing ground to patrol south of the Isle of Wight. Word had it that something was afoot. We were airborne fifteen minutes, circling some twenty miles out to sea when, in the distance to the east, German aircraft were sighted heading for the English coast. We turned and gave chase. The Huns wheeled away and eluded us, turning eastward towards France and out of range.

One lone aircraft unaware of our existence was later observed flying straight and level slogging slowly inland towards Britain. Within a short space of time a medium bomber JU 188, unlucky to find a Typhoon squadron airborne, was lying a horrible wreck in a field close to the Solent. On landing we were taken to view the wreckage. I had never witnessed such a mess of destruction, death and damage at close range. We stood speechless, nothing hostile in our shared silence, gazing at the appalling sight. The Junkers 188 normally flew with a crew of four, but at a glance this aircraft had more than four dead bodies entangled among the bits and pieces of the aircraft. The remains were picked up and literally shovelled aboard an open lorry in a mangled mess and transported by a tumbrel back to the medical centre, a marquee separate from our domestic site. There they were unloaded. A number of us watched stoically as a burly red-faced police sergeant proceeded to handle formless pieces which were placed together as they slid off the tilted lorry.

Enveloped in an odious smell, this large country bobby re-arranged these portions of raw flesh and broken bones in an attempt to complete whole bodies. He succeeded seven times over. The only thing alive and ticking was the pilot's watch. It was later confirmed that the aircraft and its seven crew members were defecting, but were very unlucky to have selected such an inopportune moment.

I was interviewed for Commissioning at the beginning of April 1944. Returning from leading a section of four aircraft on an early morning raid at Abbeville, I was invited on landing to report to Air Vice Marshal McEvoy, awaiting my presence in the officers' mess marquee. We spent half an hour together during which time he asked for pertinent and detailed accounts of my operational experiences together with some other general questions.

Three weeks later on 1 May 1944, as 177078 Pilot Officer Kyle, I moved my belongings from one tent to another. I left the 'need to know' parameters of the sergeants' mess and entered into a honeypot of operational news, subtlety and intrigue. Such was the officers' mess. I simply took off my sergeant's stripes, fitted a thin pilot officer band to the shoulder strap of my battledress and strolled in. I felt marvellous. New

Newly commissioned on 1 May 1944

uniforms and other clothing were necessary and a day off
enabled me to visit London and one of the well-known West
End tailors, not grudging the expense. Staying overnight, I took
in a cinema and a throbbing half hour at a strip club. Then I
strolled in to Shepherd's Mayfair Pub, a well-known haunt of
aircrew looking for company. The wailing of sirens and
muffled explosions were heard in the distance later that night,
as the buzz-bombs fell on London.

Coincidentally, news of promotion to warrant officer came
through the same day as my commission, which was precisely
two years since Texas and, to really make 1 May a day to
remember, I was informed that I had been awarded the
Distinguished Flying Medal. The convivial celebration cost
me twenty-nine pints, one for each member of the squadron,
plus extras. The celebrations carried on well into the evening
and now that I was being paid 21s 6d per day, I felt I could
afford it.

Wing Commander Baker was a tall fair-haired handsome
character with a typical wartime flowing RAF moustache and
the appropriate call sign of 'Lochinvar'. He had a happy-go-
lucky personality, full of animated anecdotes and a passion for
words, caring more for the expression for its own sake rather
than its substance. It made great and enjoyable listening.

We nicknamed him 'Young Lochinvar'; a brave and
glamorous knight among us. We all loved his flamboyant
personal force and delightful character. His influence inspired
laughter, enthusiasm and confidence, and did much to create a
very high standard of morale throughout the whole of the
operational unit, for both air and ground personnel.

How we missed him and his leadership, his formidable
presence, and his infectiously convivial company in the bar in

The wreckage and grave of Wing Commander Reg Baker at Beny-sur-Mer, Normandy

the evenings. He went missing, presumed killed, soon after D-Day, meeting his destiny in Normandy. It is reported he dived to his death reporting in a calm, confident voice for the wing to turn 180 degrees out of the intense flak. Using the wing call sign, he called: 'port 180 – Lochinvar out.'

Many other gregarious and carefree personalities fell by the wayside, some posthumously honoured. Even though I can't recall their names, to someone, somewhere, they will always be remembered. Daily we were vulnerable and conscious of the nearness of death. The recurring fatalities made it almost tangible. Thus some of us changed. Striving to immunize ourselves from the strains of war we became new harder selves, cynical and callous, and not only with our adversaries. There were instances when enquiries from friends and relatives gave glaring examples of our growing inhumanity. The phone would ring at an inopportune moment and an anxious voice would enquire of someone's safe return. The laconic reply 'He's not here; hard luck' worsened into either 'He's been shot down' (or 'has baled out/crash landed/is in the drink/is missing') or, the awful finality, 'he's dead'. Not a single word helped soften the blow. There was little time for courtesy.

Generally the atmosphere at dispersal and in the messes was brimming with confidence and the kill/loss factor barely affected morale. Losses were occurring daily but we got used to them. There was little time or inclination to brood. We looked at it this way: the war would go on and it could be your turn next. The relief of not having 'bought it' today was kept strictly private. The 'couldn't care less' attitude did not truly mirror one's personal feelings.

However, there were deeply poignant moments of emotion when one returned from an operational sortie to a shared room, where the missing comrade's possessions were still very much in evidence. Memories of good times shared soon

Part of my Log Book entry for July 1944

dissolved, as bitter thoughts that he was now either lodged in
the bed-rocks of the English Channel, or embedded deep in a
hole in the foreign fields of France, trapped in the cockpit of
his wrecked Typhoon. For him never to be seen again was
unbelievable. That trauma I often witnessed but thankfully
seldom experienced, as I shared a room with Len for most of
the war.

The night was still dark and stormy at 4.30 am. The wind and
rain lashed the tent as I climbed, steel-helmeted, out of my
canvas bed, donned my battledress and proceeded to the met.
briefing with thirty other pilots. The previous evening the mess
had bristled with expectation but a storm had raged unabated
for the past twenty-four hours. The forecast was still bad and I
was sceptical about whether or not we would go this time.

The wind was howling and the rain beat down as two
squadrons of Typhoon fighter-bombers, fully armed, taxied out
for take-off. At 0615 hours I was airborne. We formed up in
tight formation and coasted out at 900 ft in poor weather
conditions, and set heading for our target at Bayeux, a small
town just inside the Normandy coast. Immediately the wheels
of my aircraft left the ground I was confronted by an almost
unbelievable panorama of ships of all shapes and sizes grouped
closely together as far as the eye could see. The armada-like
stream of naval traffic in the Solent and across the Channel was
maintained over the whole hundred miles to the French coast.
The Isle of Wight was surrounded and appeared as if it was
being towed out to sea. What a spectacle it was to us. Flying
low over this continuous stream of ships, the sea looked bad
and I spared a thought for those on board. Approaching the
French coast we saw the morning sky alight with rocket
salvoes, a bombardment from the mightiest naval armada ever

assembled in the history of warfare. We could feel the drama that was unfolding that day.

The long awaited invasion of the Continent had begun. The Allies had set sail to storm the Nazi fortress of Europe. The great day of decision had arrived. 'You are about to embark upon a great crusade', said General Eisenhower. It was D-Day, 6 June 1944. A date that will be remembered for countless years. The massive number of shells exploding on the blazing beaches seemed so remote and unreal as we crossed inbound at 0640 hours about 500 ft, the maximum the cloud base and visibility would allow. We cruised quickly up to target, a German High Command headquarters. Buzzing around at 300 mph, bombing and strafing at will, the chateau was soon in ruins. There was little opposition and only a small amount of concentrated light flak was noticeable. We departed after twenty minutes, our mission successfully completed for that morning. But action was not yet over. On coasting out

James Kyle in his Typhoon approaching the Beachhead over landing craft at 0640 hrs on D-Day, 6 June 1944. From a painting by military artist John Batchelor

homeward bound at 1,500 ft, due to the vagaries of the weather the cloud base lifted a little. I was astonished and annoyed to witness more flak whizzing past me in all directions, especially as it appeared to be arriving from our own troops on the beach-head. Having stormed the beaches, they had managed to get some guns ashore and as we did look like German FW 190 fighter aircraft in the gloom of the morning, maybe excuses can be made for trigger-happy soldiers. But it was cold comfort for us being fired upon even under those circumstances. Fortunately not one of our aircraft was hit. No one became a victim of our own forces in this instance, but certain misunderstandings did occur later.

Once again we headed north in loose battle formation, feeling relaxed and confident, viewing the vast array of ships still sailing onward towards the beach-head. Thinking about and imagining the thoughts of the men aboard, I wondered how and when it would all end. All our wing aircraft landed safely back at our tented base, quickly refuelled and were again available for the next assault on the beach-head, wherever it might be. It wasn't long before the squadron was airborne again and that time they weren't so fortunate. Luckily I wasn't with them.

My first trip after D-Day was when the squadron was on an armoured reconnaissance in the Lisieux area to the east of Caen. We were flying at 1,500 ft and I was leading the flight on the starboard side. We had complete flexibility of movement, as it was a Rhubarb seek and destroy operation, with no special target designated. The squadron had been airborne some thirty minutes, having coasted in west of Caen and were now heading due east. Looking out to my right I spotted a long, broad, white concrete road, with a whole battalion of marching men and machines. Staff cars were passing back and forth along the line of troops.

Being in charge of the starboard section I called the squadron Commander:

'Blue one to Red Leader, target at two o'clock.'

I stated my observations and asked permission to attack with my number two only. The request was granted. Calling blue two to follow me we peeled off to the right, diving low towards the road. Sweeping round to the right and behind, then turning left, I positioned to arrive very low and lined up for a long strafing attack along the broad highway. We flew in close together, guns blazing along the columns of marching men as we swept the area. The soldiers went down like ninepins. Some jumped for cover into ditches as we roared past at head level. Making a very tight turn we continued strafing with another run in the opposite direction, picking off tanks, trucks and anything that remained mobile.

A staff car had stopped. I observed officer occupants alighting and running for cover under a nearby tree. I noted this as I flashed past at tree-top level and turned for a further and final attack, opening up on the staff car, then banking slightly left to get the tree as well. On flashing past I turned sharp right, looking down at the turmoil, then climbed away rocking my wings as a rejoining signal to Nobby Clark, my number two, before reunion with the squadron. It had been a most exciting 'beat up', albeit a quick one. Most of my ammunition was spent; the remainder was nonchalantly let off at a water tower near the coast as we headed for home. Other sections of the squadron had also been active during the sweep. None of our aircraft suffered damage, as there were no enemy fighters and there had been little retaliating fire from the ground – such was the confusion of the enemy, who were then on the run.

It was established later through intelligence that on this sortie of ours a German general had been killed along with a number of staff officers. Also at this time came the statement made by the German Army Staff that the strafing attacks were nigh unbearable and were adversely affecting the morale of troops. It was no longer 'Achtung Spitfire' but 'Achtung Typhoon'.

It had been a successful mission for our squadron, claiming a variety of targets destroyed. A 'wizard show' all round, I noted in my log book.

It is sad to relate that Nobby Clark, who we had jammed into a jeep the previous evening for a night out on the town, a night of bawdy choruses and blurred impressions, was to be killed. He had lasted longer than most of the original members of the squadron, and could have had only a few more months to go before the end of his first tour. So another friend perished, but by now one was getting hardened to people not coming back.

For thirty days after the invasion we operated from our temporary landing strip at Needs Ore Point, from the nearby Hurn/Bournemouth airport and from advance bases B15 and B3 on the beach-head. We stayed overnight on several occasions, due to operational necessity or to stop taking the long haul back across the channel.

From D-Day plus one we attacked and destroyed in adverse weather conditions ammunition dumps, armed camps, enemy tanks, MT vehicles, W/T trucks and gun positions. Each pilot claimed hits, either 'flamers' or 'smokers', leaving behind debris and confusion. The attacks continued. We fitted our Typhoons either with two 500 lb bombs or with one bomb and one long range tank. That meant we could penetrate many miles behind enemy lines to attack supply routes, which were either open or hidden by lines of trees. Vehicles would stop abruptly and occupants emerged to find immediate cover. We attacked enemy aircraft on the ground, anything that looked like a German headquarters, and in fact anything that moved.

Flying twice a day when the atrocious weather relented, our Ramrods and Rhubarbs at Caen, Bayeux and beyond made this period of the war hard; and still there was more to come.

On 10 June I was hit by intense flak while strafing gun positions at Argentan and on the 12th we lost Squadron Leader Fokes of 257 Squadron. On the 16th we lost Wing Commander Baker and later that day Pilot Officer Jack Watson. Squadron Leader Ross of 193 squadron and also Pilot Officer Nobby Clark were also missing by that time and many others had lost their lives. During that month, as a pilot officer I signed my own log book as the officer commanding 'B' Flight. I wondered where all the flight lieutenants had gone. Squadron leader Allan Smith (NZ) joined us as our fifth CO. He was to be shot down before the year was out and taken prisoner of war.

I awoke to the thumping of heavy gunfire. I stepped out of my tent and looked up at the early morning sky. Soon enough I would be up there. The squadron had moved across the Channel to St Croix (B3) on the beach-head, one of the many advanced landing strips. The beach-head was by then about 50 miles long and about 10 miles wide. Fifty landing strips had been carved out and prepared to take both British and American aircraft. We moved to the one at St Croix a month after D-Day. Our logistic support units were already installed there as we flew in on a permanent basis.

The site was rough and ready, the heat and the noise oppressive. The swirling dust created by Typhoons caused many problems, as it entered the engine through the large open radiator grill. To deflect dust and light sandy soil, some steel plates were invented and fitted. But our engineering and

Allan Smith

servicing teams had a long arduous task to keep these aircraft airworthy. Undercarriages were also a problem with constant take-offs and landings on the rough temporary surface causing serious malfunctions and a number of crash landings. In addition there were many flak hits that had to be patched up, but our ground crew were great and we kept flying.

The Allied armies, rapidly increasing in men and weaponry via the specially prefabricated 'Mulberry Harbours, were now firmly established on the beach-head but still battling for supremacy along the bomb-line at Caen, and other strongholds. To the west were Americans, to the east Canadians, Polish and British. We found ourselves in the unenviable position of having German guns to the front while to the left and right of us, and behind and around us was our own Allied heavy artillery. We were the 'pig in the middle' and felt somewhat insecure.

We slept under canvas or in the slit trenches we helped to dig nearby. We slept fully dressed to be readily available should anything happen, steel helmets lying loosely on or near our heads and revolvers under our pillows; I also carried a six-inch dagger tucked into my right flying boot. Fortunately it was never used in anger. We adapted to these conditions as confident young men do. The uproar and noise level at night was incredible, perhaps too high for our mental good health. After a while the lack of sleep affected efficiency and our well-being. Sometimes we felt sick from fatigue and overtiredness, and for all our bravado and carefree attitude dark charcoal rings under our eyes told of the strain some of us were facing.

The intensity of close support cab rank activities made our adrenalin flow in torrents. Risks were there in abundance each time we crossed the bomb-line. Our sorties were short in time; the flak was worse than ever, thick and accurate. The shells were exploding everywhere and the expression 'My dear, the flak' was commonplace at debriefing. We took off in flights of four, sometimes eight, and climbed rapidly to the north of the base, circling the coastline at 10,000 ft in line astern, awaiting the call from a ground liaison officer, usually a pilot, or from an Auster Recce spotting aircraft which the army used to locate and direct fire on to enemy positions. The army used red smoke signals to indicate positions, concentrated strong points, troop movements, tanks or gun sites that might be holding up an advance. We dived to Armageddon – at least some of us did. The targets for Typhoons would be passed by R/T. The controller passed map grid references on which we acted without delay. If we couldn't pinpoint the particular target allocated, anything the other side of the narrow belt which was the bomb-line was considered to be a legitimate target. We never returned fully armed. We crossed the massive light flak belt at 8,000 ft, attacked at the earliest moment, either dive-bombing or making a low level delay bomb run with all guns blazing, strafing until the ammunition was gone. We were back on the ground and the aircraft turned round, all within thirty minutes.

These short, fierce flak-ridden sorties were sweating minutes of fear that generated adrenalin and hectic tension two or three times daily. It surprised us at times that when we landed our hands were occasionally trembling and the lips decidedly dry from unconscious fear and excitement, or both. Sometimes there was insufficient time to be frightened. From our temporary airstrip in the evening and through the night we could watch part of the desperate battle for Caen, which lay battered, beleaguered, smoking and on fire in the valley below. The sound of the guns were muffled until some of the 88 mm shells lobbed perilously near with loud unexpected cracking noises that shook the tents. A few vehicles scattered around the area were hit but no aircraft.

Some of us managed to visit Caen by truck soon after its capture. We were appalled and concerned at the destruction and gruesome sights caused by incessant bombing by aircraft and heavy artillery. Due to the enemy's strong defence it was the most concentrated and the heaviest damage inflicted anywhere near the beach-head. As we drove in, I noticed a gendarme, supposedly controlling traffic at a cobbled cross-road, casually relieve himself where he stood. Bayeux, on the other hand, was almost untouched when a number of us visited the town to view the tapestry, that magnificent strip of embroidery, wool on linen, and over 250 feet long, telling the story of the Norman Conquest, now 1,000 years old. The story of the Normandy beach-head and Allied conquest will probably last as long.

Unexpectedly one morning we were summoned to a corner of the airfield. We formed up casually and were thrilled to see

Winston Churchill on a visit to the beach-head in July 1944. He is surrounded by officers and men of 146 wing on B3 near Caen

a man standing on a temporary platform. Winston Churchill had paid us a visit. In the high wind and open air his voice didn't sound as strong and sonorous as we had come to know it over the radio. He said a few words that were difficult to hear, but his presence was sufficient to convey the spirit of victory.

The Americans had captured Cherbourg with its excellent harbour, and had made the break out of the Normandy peninsula, sweeping south-east and outflanking Caen. Our squadrons were attacking road and rail bridges ahead in the Argentan and Falaise Gap area, at the request of Army operations. Eighteen Bombphoons, as we had come to call our aircraft, were involved.

Arriving overhead, milling around at 3,000 or 4,000 ft, identifying targets and awaiting my turn to dive, I noticed low to the right a squadron of rocket Typhoons hammering away at something in the valley. The flashing rockets were streaking like glowing arrows to the target as each aircraft fired its salvo. A thought crossed my mind that I was thankful I was flying a Bombphoon. We were less vulnerable than those fitted with rocket rails, because when our bombs had gone we were once again a fighter. I remember that vulnerable feeling when escorting a number of American Boston and Marauder aircraft. We were saddled with bombs slung under the wings and had flaps down to contain our speed within that of the bombers. We were tied to the bombers, and were sitting ducks for enemy fighters. Some of those rocket Typhoon pilots, with their restricted manoeuvrability thought likewise.

My turn came to dive that day and I attacked with my number two, Flight Sergeant Jack Watson. I released the two delay bombs, and simultaneously fired the four 20 mm cannons. I had anticipated the shudder that would vibrate throughout the aircraft, but was startled and shocked as a terrific bang came from the rear. I thought immediately I had blown myself up or been struck by debris, or the delay had failed and that the bombs had exploded immediately beneath me. With an odd sensation of suspense in the pit of my stomach I imagined half my tailplane blown away. Continuing for a few seconds with the attack run, I pulled up and away, undecided whether to bale out or try to make it back to base. Luckily I was still airborne, but with severe rumblings throughout the aircraft. Being rather loath and also really too low to bale out, I decided to streak back and make my escape over the bomb-line to the landing strip if possible. Coming in on a wing and a prayer, with sloppy controls, I anxiously made it and landed safely. Fate had relented.

Checking the aircraft after landing, 20 mm cannon shells were discovered embedded in the wing and tailplane; some of them had not exploded. The thudding and the extra loud bang from the rear had been caused by those shells that my number two had fired too soon from too close. My immediate thoughts, among others were that unprintable, was that it was dangerous enough coping with the enemy, avoiding flak, fighters and other hazards without having to contend with this sort of unpardonable negligence.

I expressed my disapproval in no mean fashion with a fluency of lucid acrimonious remarks and intemperate language that astounded me. This was followed by an icy distant and strained relationship for the remainder of the day with me gravitating to the opposite end of the combined marquee mess. Gradually the passion cooled and we settled it amicably, but that unnecessary close encounter had upset me. The result of the on-the-spot squadron inquiry produced a reprimand, but after an interval, a day, we were flying together again, the incident forgiven but not forgotten.

Jack Watson, a Geordie, with a small scruffy fair moustache and a stubborn streak, was not the ace of the base but a good steady pilot with lots of guts and impervious to fear. He was soon, however, to make a further and fatal error, sacrificing his life on a similar mission. He committed the cardinal sin, something of which we were all aware, of diving towards the target for far too long, and completing an unintentional Kamikaze attack by sheer concentration on target.

A number of weeks before I was due to finish my operational tour a vacancy came through from Command Administrative Headquarters for a pilot to be nominated and sent on a week's rest course. Not one pilot on the squadron was interested. No one wanted to leave the beach-head at that crucial period of the war. However, one pilot had to go and the squadron medical officer nominated me. I complained vigorously. Send one of the new arrivals I said, but the doctor considered that the unremitting daily stress and continuous missions were having an effect on my nervous system. The strain and attrition of battle were showing and the squadron commander agreed, stating that as I was nearing the end of my tour it was best that I should go. I was more exhausted than I realized.

I flew across to England as a passenger in an Anson aircraft. It felt strange that first time sitting in a plane doing nothing, so totally different from my usual type of flying. After landing at several aerodromes en route we eventually reached RAF Northolt, from where I made my way by train to East Grinstead on the Sussex Downs. I arrived at a beautiful and palatial country mansion, with large grounds and tended lawns. The house was surrounded by huge towering beeches, oaks and elms and extensive dense shrubberies. Stepping inside I was confronted with sumptuous furnishings and the architecture of a bygone age. The beautiful house had a wainscoted spiral staircase, heavy candelabra hanging from the ceiling, and handsome balustrades. It was impressive and provided extraordinary accommodation, food, wine and excellent service. Twenty more pilots, a mixed bunch of nationalities, but mainly New Zealanders and Canadians, arrived that same day.

Famous people and celebrities turned up daily, and after an introduction and discussion at tea an evening dinner party was the norm. One evening, to our pleasant surprise, the film star Major Clark Gable came to dinner. He had just completed operational trips as a trained air gunner with the American Strategic Air Force in Flying Fortresses.

He was accompanied by the English actress Elizabeth Allen, and a few pretty senior nurses from the nearby Queen Victoria Hospital at East Grinstead, made famous by the incredible medical feats accomplished there. Clark Gable was a well-built character, seemingly bigger off than on screen. He was

Film star Clark Gable with Elizabeth Allen and senior staff of the Queen Victoria Hospital at East Grinstead, where extraordinary feats of plastic surgery were performed. The author (standing third from right) is in his Texas jumper

surprisingly modest and quietly spoken. It was a pleasure to meet him.

After dinner the party developed along the usual lines. We spent some time talking shop, lavishly embellishing line shoots and drinking until some of us needed to be more active. As high-spirited and relaxed young men, all in good voice, full of health, vitality and with an excess of energy, we made the best of the five days away from the war zone.

I recall sliding down those handsome curved banisters and shooting off the end on to a pile of bodies already entangled on the floor. In the frolic one New Zealander 'went for a Burton' through the second-floor window. His fall was broken by a partially pollarded elm tree and a towering oak. He landed drunkenly on his feet to run in and rejoin the fray. Invariably each evening was a great success. The rest proved therapeutic in every sense. Soon it was all over and I returned to Normandy, back to the fray and to the final phase of the war.

The end of my war on Typhoons ended sooner than I expected. Notification of posting and the end of my first operation tour arrived. It possibly surprised the postings staff, as few Typhoon pilots had managed to complete a full tour of operations. That penultimate week was crowded with a frenzy of flying before destiny ordained that I did no more operational missions. My Typhoon tour concluded, I said my goodbyes and grudgingly left the squadron, inhibited by deep emotion and a feeling of loss difficult to explain.

I had flown Typhoons incessantly for almost two years, and had grown to love and respect the aircraft. They had served me well. I had always felt comfortable and confident in the cockpit and at the controls, and I had had none of the problems that plagued both plane and pilots. To recall the bang and roar of the engine as I pressed the cartridge starter, to smell the petrol, hydraulic oil and acrid odours as I sat in the hot sun in the cockpit, to sniff cordite smoke from the cannons and to sense the beautiful sensation of scrambled take-offs low across the green airfields: those nostalgic memories of a wonderful environment remain with me to this day. I remember too the intense excitement and scent of danger in incidents when life or death hung by split-second timing, or instinct or sheer intuition, by innate good judgement or just good luck.

I was amazed at my own destiny. I had the capacity and luck to survive and was seemingly indestructible. I had that feeling during this immortal adventure that something or perhaps someone, some guardian angel, was steering me through the danger, guiding me to turn the right way at the right time. Maybe I was just plain lucky. Maybe I had nine lives. Someone said 'only the able man has luck', but it was more than just good fortune that kept me alive while others around me fell.

During my period with the squadron only five of the original members who formed the squadron at Drem, Scotland in 1942 managed to remain alive; two were from 'A' Flight and three of us from 'B' Flight. We went through five wing leaders, five squadron leaders and five times five pilots during those twenty months. Of the five that survived all were decorated, but again the will of fate played its hand and the two remaining pilots of 'B' Flight were killed in flying accidents shortly after the war. And so there was one. I was lucky, and so it continued.

My six years of flying from Texas in 1941 until demobilization at the end of the war shows in my log book as a total of 1,000 hours on single engine aircraft, a most exacting amount. Almost 400 hours were on my favourite aircraft, the fearsome Typhoon.

The following comments were entered in my log book: 'This officer has just completed an eighteen month tour of operations. He has shown great keenness and performed his duties in a courageous manner. He is a good leader and I assess him as above the average.' Remarks of a similar kind were applicable to most pilots who survived the operational exploits of the Second World War in 197 and all Typhoon Squadrons.

CHAPTER 7

The Flight of Time

My orders were to report to No. 55 OTU at RAF Aston Down, near Stroud in the Cotswolds, Gloucestershire. I asked a ticket collector at Paddington station where Stroud was located. He replied: 'I haven't a clue.' I boarded the train and arrived in Stroud in due course.

Posted from the invasion force and the beach-head I returned to Britain for a statutory six months' rest period. My task was to convert pilots of the popular Spitfire to the dreaded Typhoon. Many of these Spitfire pilots were less than exuberant, some totally disillusioned, while others had an aversion to their new brute of an aircraft, showing their feelings in no mean language. The Spitfire was no longer necessary for fighter sweeps and war in the air had been won, but there was still much to be done with the low level fighter-bomber. So for six months at Aston Down in the Cotswolds I flew weather checks, air tests, instructed in dive-bombing, rocket-firing techniques and leading formations around the sky.

In a short detachment to RAF Wing, Bucks, I was sent to fly Hurricanes on night-fighter affiliation to give practice and training for Bomber Command air gunners. The Hurricane this time round felt like a toy in my hands and I made the most of it, rolling around the circuit at 500 ft, side-slipping and landing from the top of a loop, turning on a sixpence. Its manoeuvrability was marvellous, making one appreciate why it did so well in the Battle of Britain. Slightly slower than the Spitfire and the ME 109, it could out-turn both of its more glamorous rivals. The air gunners at the school were apprehensive when

they found out that a certain P/O Kyle was the Hurricane pilot.
I got close enough on the attack to see the whites of their eyes,
whereupon they would stop functioning the guns and cower
back as I yanked hard back on the stick, skimming the tailplane
for a zoom climb and upward roll. This flying was different
and enjoyable, but I longed to be back on operations before the
war ended. I felt I was wasting my time. One night when sitting
alone in my aircraft at 31,000 ft, passing time, infernally cold,
feet and fingers almost frozen, the aircraft hanging by the
propeller, with the rate of climb indicator reading zero, I looked
up into the starry sky receding into infinity, then down to the
dark void below, broken by only isolated dimmed street
lighting. In the solitude and silence of the night amid the
immensity and splendour of the stars, I thought to myself:
'What in hell am I doing up here?' It was a curious uncanny
sensation, a slight eeriness, a feeling of isolation and
remoteness that only a lone pilot can experience when stooging
about, filling in time in the middle of the night at high altitude.
The Hurricane detachment was over and I returned to flying the
Typhoon. I was now awaiting the next operational posting as
my rest period was ending.

During that six months' rest period in the Cotswolds I met and
married Jean at the local church in Stroud on St Patrick's Day
in 1945. We spent the first two years apart while I served in
Germany, but have now been together for forty-eight years and
will soon celebrate our golden wedding anniversary.

The new posting arrived and I was delighted with it. I was to
join a front-line fighter squadron and proceed immediately to

Marriage to Jean on St Patrick's Day, 1945, in Stroud

The Tempest Mk V – so beautiful to fly (RAF Museum, Hendon)

a Tempest conversion unit. The war in Europe ended just a few days before my arrival on the squadron but rumour had it that we would soon be en route to the Far East. Hopes were raised once more but they dropped the bomb from the B29 'Enola Gay' on Hiroshima on 6 August 1945. The war was over. The defeat of the Axis forces was almost complete; only one more bomb at Nagasaki was needed a few days later.

I joined No. 80 Tempest fighter squadron at Fassberg aerodrome in Germany directly after the war ended. No. 80 squadron was one of the oldest squadrons of the RAF, their squadron badge was a bell and their motto was 'Strike True'. They were formed during the First World War with Camel-type aircraft, progressing through the years to Gladiators, Hurricanes, Spitfires and Tempests. The Tempest was similar in flying characteristics to the Typhoon except that it was a little lighter on the controls, more manoeuvrable, faster and more exciting to handle. The wings were shaped towards the

"JIMMIE".

James Kyle sketched by cartoonist Pat Rooney in Germany

Spitfire profile, also thinner and stronger than the Typhoon. A slick good-looking aircraft, and so beautiful to fly.

No. 80 squadron had been one of the first squadrons to be equipped with Tempests, along with No. 3, 56 and 486 NZ Squadron. Their main task was chasing the V1 pilotless aircraft, named the 'Doodle Bug' by the New Zealanders, which were launched from the Pas de Calais area, and by day and night indiscriminately fell on London, and towns on the south coast.

Flying at over 450 mph the Tempest was capable of closing with the flying bomb. The technique employed was to be positioned about 2,000 ft above, on patrol or to be scrambled awaiting their arrival, then diving from behind to quickly overtake, and either shoot the bomb down or catch it up and, by touching wings, cheekily tip it over, out of harm's way. Some pilots got too close before firing, consequently flying through the debris of the explosion and causing damage to themselves and the aircraft, but this was soon remedied and the Tempest proved very successful in this unusual role.

Fassberg aerodrome lay close to the Belsen concentration camp and a hidden single-line railway ran direct from a corner of the airfield to the camp. I took that line with others that first evening on arrival at Fassberg, to view the wire enclosure and black remains of the buildings where appalling scenes of deliberate slaughter, hunger, overt brutality, gassings and exterminations took place. A sense of discomfort pervaded the whole atmosphere; it was depressing to behold. Clear in our minds was the concept of what was meant by the 'final solution'. We departed contemplating with a sense of shivery fear what might have happened if Hitler had won the war. The

Memorial at Belsen concentration camp, 1945

Holocaust might have been repeated on an even larger scale throughout the world.

The squadron moved from Fassberg soon after my arrival but not before I was given the opportunity to fly a German aircraft. Some gliders needed to be delivered to Schleswigland in northern Germany, and I was delighted to be the pilot nominated for the towing. I flew the Focke-Wulf FW 56, a high-winged open cockpit monoplane capable of short take-offs and landings somewhat similar to the Westland Lysander. I completed a couple of quick circuits and landings in this 240 hp engine aircraft just to get the feel of it before the long haul north. The cockpit instruments were in metric units and all flying speeds required a quick conversion to miles per hour, (halve it and add a quarter). The layout was the opposite way round to that of British aircraft and even the pungent smell of the cockpit was different. It must have been the sauerkraut. I flew the route twice towing the gliders.

James Kyle on the tail of a JU88 in northern Germany, 1945

To overfly the devastated bombed-out cities of Hamburg and Kiel and other smaller towns of the Fatherland was an odd experience. As I flew back and forth on those four journeys it seemed strange to look down and reflect that what was once invincible was now in great waste and ruins. I wondered how long it would take to rebuild, and whether it could ever happen again.

From Fassberg the squadron moved direct to Copenhagen soon after the liberation of the Danish capital. We flew into and operated from Kastrup aerodrome for the next three months. As in Texas, the family hospitality was sincere and overflowing. It was a period of wild parties and non-stop horseplay, with intermittent bouts of flying. I remember standing on my head during a balancing act at a party, attempting to consume a bottle of Danish schnapps while trying to enunciate one of their more difficult expressions, 'strawberries and cream'. The days and nights of drinking schnapps and pints of black velvet took their toll. Many of us suffered badly, becoming either totally incapacitated or simply shattered and exhausted. I ended up in the hospital with a suspected hiatus hernia. They fed me tinned chicken, milk and ice cream for three days.

Flying was sporadic. It had temporarily lost some of its appeal, even though flying around the green islands and lakes of Denmark was delightful. What we lacked and missed was the implicit danger associated with operational flying; it was a bore to some pilots. Besides, there were other more tantalizing distractions.

On the days we flew in earnest we engaged in many dogfights, each one of us endeavouring to outgun the other. We gained the crucial element of surprise by attacking from high above and out of the sun, thereby demonstrating our unchanged will to win.

Just landed and switched off at Kastrup, Copenhagen, 1945

Germany, 1945: leaning on the prop on leaving the cockpit. My aircraft W2-X is in the background

Part of the Battle of Britain first flypast in 1945. Douglas Bader is leading

Twenty minutes or so of the sheer delight of the friendly dogfights and we were ready to land, our flying commitment over for the day. From this type of flying we went to the other extreme, and embarked on low-level interception and navigational sorties to keep us mentally fit and fully prepared.

We had one commanding officer who was invariably inebriated. He did no flying other than a quick solo trip. At a party once, I remember one chap helping me, each of us with a leg, to drag the CO down two flights of stairs, the back of his poor head slapping against every stone step on the way back to his bedroom. Surprisingly he was particularly bright the next morning and, to prove it, went flying. He was a little round the bend.

Pilots at Sylt, 1946

Pilots in a Jeep, Sylt 1946

In September 1945 we flew from Copenhagen to RAF
Manston to participate in the Battle of Britain fly-past, directly
behind war hero Douglas Bader. With the time difference and a
strong tail wind we landed our Tempests at Manston before the
hour we left from Kastrup. It was a memorable event lasting
three days. My wife, whom I had barely seen since our marriage,
joined me at Margate. The dance hall of 'Dreamland' was a
welcome change from the drunken excursions in Copenhagen.

I remained with No. 80 Squadron for two years as we hopped
throughout Germany, to aerodromes at Lübeck, Schleswig-

Holstein, the nudist island of Sylt, Gatow, Berlin and eventually to a permanent base at Wunstorf, near Hanover. There I spent my leisure hours sailing on the Steinhuder Meer and skiing on the slopes of the Harz Mountains.

I was a flight commander at Wunstorf. A year previously I had been granted a one year extension while awaiting the result of my application for a permanent commission in the RAF. I desperately wanted to remain in the service but, like many of my friends, expected that I would be passed over for selection. My suspicions held true, as it did for hundreds of others. I was shattered and insulted by the denial.

Unfortunately I was due to fly. Upon receiving the depressing news, I jumped into a Tempest and took to the sky in a savage, foul temper. I proceeded to 'beat up' the aerodrome. After a hair-raising thirty minutes of unrelenting aerobatics and high speed runs, grazing the grass and hangar roof-tops, pulling white streamers from the wings with every turn, I landed and returned to the dispersal only to find myself

The Tempest MK 11 with the radial engine, which I flew in Berlin in 1946

The author aged twenty-five, 1946

challenged by the squadron commander. He was not pleased. We were not always as one; I was indifferent to his authority and there was a marked animosity and tension between us.

'Jimmy,' he stated severely, 'you will not beat up the airfield like that again. The war is over. You must and will control yourself.'

Glaring angrily at him, incapable of self-restraint, I glibly told him to 'f— off in a fine pitch'. I couldn't have cared less. Hitching my parachute higher up on my shoulder I strutted off, totally demoralized.

Subsequently my tour and wartime commission expired.

Flying Mosquito aircraft at Schleswigland for the NATO armies in the Baltic, 1957

CHAPTER 8

Highlights from later life

In June 1947 I was posted back to England for demobilization, after my request to stay in the RAF permanently had been refused. Leaving the service's cocoon of security to start a new life was indeed a challenge. A peacetime occupation to match the excitement of the war years was going to be difficult to find.

I decided to settle with my wife and small daughter, Denise, in the Cotswolds, near Stroud. After two month's leave I found a job as a draughtsman with a light engineering firm, and also took a correspondence course in draughtsmanship with Bennett College, Sheffield. After three years, however, the urge to fly again was overpowering, and I rejoined the RAF as a Flying Officer in January 1951.

'With BSA Scout prior to Demobilisation' in 1946

My son David had been born. I left my wife and two children at Stroud and reported to RAF Finningley in Yorkshire for a flying refresher course.

My first trip at Finningley was as the saying goes, 'a piece of cake', like riding a bike; once you can fly you can always fly. However during my absence, a new instrument flying assessment scheme had been introduced by the RAF. I found myself sadly lacking in this type of flying, having done very little on instruments during the war. Training was completed satisfactorily but I left Finningley with insufficient hours to reach an instrument rating category and was posted to Central Flying School, CFS, RAF Little Rissington to become a qualified flying instructor, QFI. In addition to Little Rissington we used the aerodromes of South Cerney, Kemble and Aston Down.

This was an intensive course of accurate flying with explanatory commentary of all actions and aspects of flight, together with ground school studies of considerable detail on pertinent subjects appertaining to flying and airmanship. It was here I began lecturing. My final assessment lecture was selected for me. I was asked unexpectedly to give a fifteen minute talk on the difference between centrifugal and centripetal force. This was quite an experience and a real struggle to survive for such a specified time on such a specific subject.

It was here at CFS I flew the Gloster Meteor, my first jet aircraft. One had to fly solo on this aircraft at the end of the course before being awarded the Qualified Instructors Certificate.

My wife and two children had joined me at Little Rissington, where we all lived in a small caravan near Bourton-on-the-Water. I passed out of No. 25 course with a 'B' category some six months later, when we then all moved to RAF Oakington, near Cambridge.

For the next year at Oakington, I instructed on Harvards, training mainly ex-Bomber Command pilots who hadn't been on their backs, (inverted flying), for five years or more. The

Jean and Jim Kyle somewhere in the Cotswolds in 1947

aerobatics were almost continuous, some by moonlight, as I had four students on each course. After my years with the Typhoon and Tempest, flying the Harvard was more of a toy. It was great fun and created a good deal of excitement amongst the students. Social life was also very enjoyable. There were many receptions and farewells with such a large turnover and influx of war-time pilots re-entering with the expansion of the RAF.

A year later RAF Oakington was allotted a different task. All of our Wing of six flights of Harvards moved. Four flights of pilots moved with all the planes to Moreton-in-Marsh and two flights of pilots went to RAF Wellesbourne Mountford, near Stratford-on-Avon, to be converted to twin engine Oxford aircraft. This was to be my first experience of twin engined piston aircraft. One instructional flight and I went solo. Later, after hours of instrument flying practice, I was appointed the Instrument Rating Examiner, IRE, for the squadron and took all student pilots on their final instrument rating test. I also flew the Station Chipmunk aircraft to give experience to some students who may be posted to single engine aircraft. This was a pleasant spell of real flying, in this little gem of an aircraft, which I looked forward to at the end of each course.

Unfortunately I came unstuck. I was authorised to fly an instructional low-level navigational cross-country exercise. Travelling at 150 knots on the second leg, I cut and flew through the main 300,000 volt electricity high tension cables between Northampton and Bedford. The sun was shining, glinting on the odd patch of snow still persisting on the ground and on the water at where the river bends in the valley. Away in the distance through the haze, a rise in the ground was evident. Checking our navigational position we flew on. The snow laden cables were slack and hanging heavy. The lower cable of four was hidden and sitting on top of the trees on an upslope. The other cables were barely visible and difficult to see from any angle. The Station Navigation Officer had decided that day, prior to and without knowledge of my accident, to place greater emphasis on briefing for this obstruction in the future.

On siting the cables at very close range, I snatched the controls of the aircraft from my student and pulled up very quickly, instinctively keeping the wings level so that the propellers cut the second cable from the top. Sparks flew off the engine, extending along the leading edge of the wings and a large hole appeared on the port side of the fuselage at my student's feet. The hole was caused by the lashing of the cables as they severed. I climbed the aircraft and tested it which seemed OK so we continued with our low-level cross country. Before landing at base, I checked the aircraft at the incipient stall stage and flew over the control tower for a visual check on the undercarriage. On landing it was apparent that the propellers had inches off their tips and the underside of the wings were scarred and damaged caused by lashings from the cables. On leaving the cockpit, I was placed under close arrest pending investigation for Court Martial. This took some weeks. However after all the evidence was gathered, the Court Marial was rescinded and I was posted to Northern Ireland. Any chance of promotion was gone. Incidently the students name was Bedford, who went on to get his wings. A few weeks later two pilots on a similar exercise turned, sat on these cables and were killed; burnt to death.

In Northern Ireland at RAF Cluntoe, County Tyrone 1953, I flew Prentice and Harvard aircraft. At least I was back on single engines again. One night whilst night flying, an escape and evasion exercise was taking place. I arranged a time and place by the side of Lough Neagh to land and pick up one of the evaders. In my Prentice aircraft I made a touch and go landing in a remote field on a rendezvous near the lake hoping to pick up my passenger; but he wasn't there. It reminded me of the task of the Lysanders at Tangmere as they carried out their dangerous esoteric excursions in Nazi occupied Normandy.

After a year in Northern Ireland, I volunteered for a specialist pilot-navigation course starting at RAF Shawbury, Shropshire. I made my way there with my wife, two kids and a caravan with the warning that if I failed the course I would be made to pay my way back to Cluntoe. With that to motivate me, I passed as a qualified navigator with an 'n' brevet, but it was a long hard slog of private study. Posted to Ternhill, which was just along the road, I was allocated a married quarter for the first time since re-entry. After attending an Instructional Technique Course, I spent three years at Ternhill instructing on pilot navigation, both on the ground and in the air. Maps and Charts and mental dead reckoning being predominate. I took all the students on their final navigation test which could be quite severe. Many of them became uncertain of their position, got all worked up and in a sweat, beads of it showing on their foreheads as they tried to establish their position accurately. There were few failures.

It was at Ternhill I took up golf. I was 35. I thought then that it was an old man's game but now I know different. I played at Market Drayton and at Hawkstone Park, a lovely course in

Shropshire. Alex Lyle was the professional, Sandy a boy of nine, was seen wielding a few irons around the practice area.

Visiting nearby RAF Cosford, I was invited to box three two minute rounds in the ring against the light weight amateur champion of Siam. He was about a stone lighter than me at around 140 lbs. There was no result but we were still on our feet at the end.

On a three day escape and evasion exercise from Ternhill, after roughing it for 48 hours and having avoided an intense manhunt by the county police and military, I was caught on the third night. At midnight, cold, hungry and in the pouring rain, I unfortunately hailed down a police car coming fast from a distance. When it got close and realising what I had done, I took off running as fast as I could go, but due to weakness of body and spirit, I was finally caught in the middle of a graveyard, taken in their car, stripped down and thrown to the floor in Nuneaton jail. I was returned to Ternhill the following day. Next morning, my daughter proudly told her teacher that her father had spent the night in Nuneaton jail.

From Ternhill in 1957 I was posted to Schleswigland in Northern Germany to fly Mosquito aircraft for the Nato armies in the Baltic. The task consisted mainly of target towing a drogue at the end of a 6000 feet cable for the combined land forces to fire at. We flew the aircraft over the sea parallel to the coast for two hours and let the soldiers have target practice. One serious incident occurred when they aimed at the aircraft instead of the drogue and nearly shot it down. The pilot of the Mosquito was more than incensed, but accepted the German excuse that it was all due to weather and a language misunderstanding. The weather at times was dreadful, snow storms quickly moving in off the Baltic sea. We had trouble with the aircraft itself. The Mosquitos were old and we thought some of the airframes were twisted because of their particular construction. With a 600 lb winch fitted underneath the fuselage they were difficult to handle on take-off.

The safety speed was 175 knots. Should anything happen below that speed whilst getting airborne the pilot would lose all directional control and the result could be fatal. In our flight of Mosquitos, we had a number of casualties of both pilots and planes.

One South African pilot had recently come from flying Vampire jets and had little experience on twin engine piston aircraft. At 30,000 feet on a cold day he stopped one engine to practice asymmetric flying. He was then unable to restart the engine. He couldn't maintain height and eventually he crash landed in the river Elbe. I was flight commander and unit QFI and was held partly to blame for the accident for giving an insufficient and inadequate asymmetric briefing to the pilot before flight. I had to travel by train from Schleswig to Munchen Gladbach for interview with the Air Officer Commanding. However on arrival, the AOC knew as well as I and all the other pilots of the flight, that the jet pilot had omitted to switch on his ignition to restart the engine. The AOC was sympathetic for my unnecessary 24 hour journey by train which was quite an ordeal in those days. The pilot never did admit to his error.

During this posting I had taken my family to Copenhagen for a short holiday. On our return there was trouble at the German-Danish border. Some men were running around waving sticks and guns and at one stage sat on the bonnet of my Mercedes, looking most menacing. Guns were fired, blood was spilled. We were all uncertain of what would happen next, but eventually the border guards got the situation under control and after a while we were allowed to drive home.

Schleswigland closed. The Mosquitos were all flown back to the UK for scrap. Once again I was posted to RAF Shawbury but this time for an introduction to the Air Traffic Control Branch and my first ground tour.

The comprehensive air traffic control course, lasting four

months, went well and I was posted to RAF Little Rissington for a busy three year ground tour. There was something déjà vu about the place. The Old New Inn, The Cheltenham racecourse and festival, Moreton-in-Marsh where my second son Jamie was born and of course the lovely Cotswold countryside made this an ideal posting. Jean, my wife is a Cotswold girl from Chalford village, near Stroud, which is just 30 miles down the road.

It was at Little Rissington I met the Queen Mother and along with Jean and others, was invited to afternoon tea. It was a pleasant and quiet interlude.

To keep in flying practice I flew the Station Chipmunk aircraft at weekends to help out with the visiting air-cadets who turned up at regular intervals. I even managed to take my son David up for a short while. 'Don't do any aerobatics Dad', he said. At that time an air show was stopped to let the new RAF Vulcan bomber make an approach, wheels and flaps down to overfly the airfield.

I was posted to Luqa, Malta. We were soon on our way overland to Malta in a heatwave. Jamie age two, had his feet stuck out the window at times to cool down. We stopped at Paris, Zurich, Rome, then sailed from Naples after a splendid two weeks holiday but not before being robbed. Fortunately my service uniform and documents were in the boot of the car. During the journey I travelled fast but was passed on the Autobahn and the Autostrada by cars that must have been doing over a ton. We stayed overnight at Bregenz on Lake Constance and watched a beautifully presented open air version of a grand opera, the stage set on the edge of the lake. Next day we went to see 'Gone with the Wind' for my family to see Clark Gable, whom I had met some sixteen years earlier and who died that year 1960.

My tour in Malta was extended to three years. My family enjoyed the beautiful climate and a new experience. My wife even managed to try to swim and dive and eventually succeeded. Daughter Denise got her three 'A' levels at the Royal Naval School, Tal Handaq. I was able to play golf every day, either

morning or afternoon depending on hours of duty. With a
handicap of 14 I made the final of the 'Creasy Cup', a major
competition of the Royal Malta Golf Club. I won £70 and bought
myself a trolley and a new set of golf clubs that I play with around
Minchinhampton today. Very recently I won a new set of Mizuno
golf clubs with bag.

From Malta, detachments with the Luqa based Canberra
Squadron flew me to Gibralter and to Áden. On the trip to Aden
I handled the controls of a VC10 as we passed over the Sudan
with what was classified as a 'Hot Load' on board. In Aden they
play golf but there is no grass. We putted on a mixture of oily
sand. On a journey to Turkey, staying overnight in Greece, I found
myself high on the Acropolis fortified hill at the Parthenon. The
city lights lay sparkling below as I watched a 2000 year old play
about Persians fighting Greeks as the Jet aircraft from Athens
airport roared overhead on a warm starlit night. A sense of the
unreal pervaded the magnificent setting.

During my air traffic control tour at Luqa, we military
controllers had to deal with civil aircraft as well as the RAF and

Picking Prickly Pears in Malta

Royal Naval aircraft based at Takali and Halfar. There could be peak periods of intense flying that kept us on our toes. What I remember most is the number of times at night that I had to rush from the control tower, jump into the jeep and drive fast in the pouring rain down the runway to the radar truck, identify the civil aircraft approaching the beacon on the island of Gozo, their pilots requesting a radar talkdown because of the extremely bad electrical storms. The equipment the Civil Airlines used was at times inaccurate under extreme weather conditions so they relied on the RAF to make a landing. We got a thank you over the R/T, but had little other contact with them.

My instructions were to report to RAF Manby, Lincs, to fly the Varsity aircraft on refresher training. Travelling back overland via Venice, The Black Forest and Brussels, six weeks later I was at RAF Stradishall, Suffolk to fly long range exercises to help train Navigators. We flew to Gibralter, Malta, El Adem, Tripoli and up over the North Sea as far as the Shetlands in atrocious weather conditions. It really could be dicey at times. I had an engine fail in icy conditions in thick cloud over the Cantabrian Mountains at Bilbao, Spain. It was really difficult to maintain height. We were skimming the mountain tops heading south but fortunately the weather cleared. On another occasion, out over the north sea, my aircraft was struck by lightning across the leading edge of the wings and along the front panel of the cockpit. It probably wasn't as bad as it looked but it was unsettling at the time.

On returning from North Africa one day, the radio compass on my aircraft became unserviceable. There was no way I could enter the French and British airways systems without it, so I landed for repairs at Nice airport. We had no money. As Captain, I organised a lift to the British Consul, told him my tale and was given some cash for the crew members to last a couple of days. We stayed overnight. Some Frenchmen gave us a welcome invite to a nightclub in Marseille. It was champagne by the bucket. We got high on this and other concoctions and were asked on the stage to join the girls doing a striptease act. A good night was had by all.

At Stradishall I took a correspondence course in Turf Accountancy. I was in Ely hospital where Hiatus Hernia was diagnosed, and which had caused me much pain over the years. They found it after twenty years of trying. My bookie's arithmetical course helped pass the time. I have a certificate which says 'strongly recommended to work as a settler in a bookie's office'. This I did later on my next posting to West Raynham in Norfolk when once again I was transferred to Air Traffic Control duties and which coincidently was to be the end of my flying career, in 1966.

At West Raynham were No. 1 Hunter Fighter Squadron. It was a Strike Command Station and I was in my element amongst the young fighter pilots who were on average half my age. There were periods of intense activity in the air and on the ground. Many pleasant evenings were spent in the Mess with my wife Jean after a hectic day of pseudo operational training exercises. There was a plethora of stories to tell in the warm glow of the bar at the end of a stressful day. One story was the sinking of the Torrey Canyon.

I was up at the crack of dawn on the 30th March 1967 to open the control tower. It was a dull morning with intermittent rain from a high stratocumulus cloud, a portend of weather to come.

Together with Sea Vixens and Buccaneers from other units, four young fighter pilots of No. 1 Hunter Fighter Squadron took off fully 'Bombed up' to attack and sink the stricken oil tanker 'Torrey Canyon'. On the 18th March 1967 the ship had run aground on the Seven Stones reef between Land's End and the Scilly Isles and was spreading its 100,000 tons of cargo along 100 miles of coastline of the English Channel and fouling the Cornish beaches.

The control tower was fully manned. All personnel were in

their respective operating positions awaiting the days flying to begin, so I took myself off to the radar truck (GCA) situated near the centre of the aerodrome. An hour later I was sitting in the grinding groaning noise of the radar equipment. Suddenly I was alerted, called into action by a crisp transmission. 'Raynham Radar Hunter Red at 35,000 feet above cloud and in the clear, requesting weather at base'. I replied sharply, giving him the ominous information. The weather had deteriorated to low cloud with heavy rain and very poor visibility underneath. Without hesitation he responded, 'Red 1, Raynham Radar, request controlled descent through cloud and GCA'. I could hear a tinge of excitement in the voice of Mick Hindley, Red Leader. I confirmed that he and his flight had dropped their bombs, strafed and fired their guns with some success. They had blasted the wreck of the oil tanker. The ship had broken up and the remainder of the source of the oil coming from the Torrey Canyon destroyed. This unusual offensive occurrence in peacetime was more than sufficient to raise the adrenalin and thrill the young fighter pilots.

To my reply on the R/T, Mick Hindley left his 'press to speak button' on and in an intake of breath said, 'Jimmy's on Radar' for his flight to hear. I felt good at his 'Jim's on' remark as it conveyed trust that can be felt under difficult flying conditions between pilots and controllers. Something I had experienced myself under more hairy circumstances. I was both radar Director and Talkdown controller in this instance. I picked them up on radar about 100 miles to the south west and gave a heading to steer to overhead base. I then turned them on to an outbound heading and requested they begin descent to reach a height suitable for pick up on the radar Talkdown display. The talkdown was satisfactory and they landed safely having descended through 35,000 feet of dreadful weather conditions in the shape of a frontal occlusion with a number of embedded cunims.

I was Station Duty Officer (SDO) that night. An exhilarating evening followed in the bar and at the piano as I extended the closing time to the early hours of the morning. All the members of the squadron and the Mess enjoyed 'High Jinks' at a spontaneous party. It was fate that I was SDO. They all knew I had fired my guns in anger when flying the fearsome Typhoon in World War II at similar targets in the English Channel. We therefore had much in common to celebrate that wet and windy day in March 1967. Later I was to go as their air traffic controller on detachment to El Adem, from where we scouted deep into the Sahara Desert.

Having taken the turf accountancy course just prior to my posting to West Raynham, I fixed myself up with some practical experience with one of the big bookmakers in Norwich, for no pay! Each Saturday would find me doing mental calculations in a busy bookie's office whilst my wife and family went shopping. On our return home we would stop at a butchers shop in Fakenham and purchase two or three massive 'T' bone steaks, for 7/6d or 37 1/2 np each. They were marvellous when grilled.

We lived at Hyde House at Bircham Newton and had a pleasant stay in our large married quarter. We had pheasants in the garden, ghosts in the squash court, golf on the links and thieves in the night. Altogether it was another interesting tour.

From West Raynham later that year I was appointed to an extensive and extended tour on the Air Traffic Control Examining Board, ATCEB, Shawbury from where I visited all the RAF Station at home and overseas except Hong Kong. This included a nostalgic duty visit to Tangmere in 1969. It was an intensive tour of travel of the UK and much of the world. Professionally it was interesting but extremely tiring living out of a suitcase week after week for three years. Lack of sleep was a real problem.

In Singapore in infamous Bughi street I was set upon by three transvestites who tried to bundle me into a taxi. Luckily I was able to fight them off and find my own taxi back to my hotel. On our visit to Gibralter the ATC equipment was unserviceable in the tower, so I managed a quick trip to Tangiers and a walk through the labyrinth of the Casbah. In GAN island in the Indian Ocean I was swooped upon by oversized bats that were active at night. In Cyprus I was photographed under the Tree of Idleness near Nicosia and often wonder why I've done very little of consequence since. My fellow examiner refused to have his picture taken and has slaved away <u>ever</u> since. My visit to Masirah and Salalah in the Sultanate of OMAN was long and tiresome. It seemed remote and unreal, as if I was living in Biblical times. At Salalah, I was asked by the station adjutant to accompany him by jeep to a port further south where a ship was unloading equipment for the unit. We were delayed and on our return were shelled by bandit tribesmen from the nearby hills. In my innocence I wasn't too concerned but I could see by the adjutant's face he thought we were in real trouble. He drove fast cowering down behind the wheel and thus we managed to get back to base safely. I was glad to get home to Shawbury and some comfort.

On returning from the Far East, one Lady on the plane was inquisitive as to who we were. We told her we are a travelling Dart Team and showed her a report I had handy on one of the Air Traffic Controllers I had examined where it said 'Has a Firm Grip!' She seemed convinced.

From the ATCEB, I left for what was to be my final posting in the RAF, Southern Radar, Sopley, near Bournemouth. I remained at Sopley for five years mainly in a supervisory capacity and I took part in the Concorde Atlantic air traffic trials from Hurn airport, played golf at Burley and became very familiar with the local area which I got to like very much indeed. I decided to live here and requested voluntary retirement. All in all I spent thirty years as a member of the Royal Air Force retired on my fifty second birthday in 1974.

Having played soccer, squash and golf in the RAF, I started jogging soon after my retirement. On 17th January 1978, age 55, on a cold black morning at 7am, I took my first steps along a trail that was to continue for seventeen years. My aim was to complete 1,000 miles in that first year and to end a five year mission with a target of 10,000.

In the beginning I began with the slowest pace at which I felt comfortable, to enable me to complete my first two miles without stopping. I continued like this for about two months and found myself getting round in 8 minutes to the mile. On the third month I increased my range to 3 miles and went a fraction faster.

In May 1978 I flew to New Orleans to visit my son David who was living and working there. He arranged for me to take part in a Gold Cup race of 5,000 metres. The weather that day was sultry and steamy, humidity 95%. I finished the course and won myself a T-shirt with badge and was pleased. I still have the shirt today, washed thin.

Later I was to visit Dallas and Denver, the mile high city, and run in the foothills of the Rockies. Jogging was difficult due to the lack of oxygen at that height, causing the lips and throat to dry, but one soon became acclimatised.

Back in the UK it was a daily run for me regardless of the weather. After six months of jogging it became a necessity, an obsession. I felt I had missed out on the day without it. The euphoria I got from jogging took me back to my flying days when I was skimming the cloud tops at high speed. Soon I was running five miles every morning and in stages reached 6, 7, 8 miles until I reached my target of 10.

In 1985 I went to Dallas to attend the first reunion of No. 1 British Flying Training School, exactly 44 years after my flying course and the attack on Pearl Harbor. It was a nostalgic event. My son David was still in the States and I was able to meet up with him again and continue our running together. We also played a little golf.

In 1987, age 65, when I was feeling good, I was approached to take part in a 10,000 metre charity race for cancer research along the South coast at Highcliffe. More than 100 others took part and it was well sponsored.

On the day of the storm, October 1987, we moved to Minchinhampton in the Cotswolds, where jogging seems to be all uphill in this undulating part of the country. Slowly but surely I'm slowing down. What I used to do in a day now takes a week. However I still have the will, more needed in the winter mornings to get out of the door. I go four mornings a week, the other three are taken up with golf. Recently I organised and luckily won a unique golf competition for the 'swinging seventies'. There were 22 of us age 70 at Minchinhampton golf course in 1992. If luck holds we hope to be doing the same thing again 10 years on, when we all stand on the brink of eighty!

Jogging on the Minchinhampton common early one Sunday morning, where there is a golf course, I was struck on the head by a stray golf ball, Immediately I thought I had had a brain hemorrhage so sudden was the pain in my head. Then I heard the ball drop. I got home soaked in blood, called the Stroud Hospital and arranged for a doctor and drove there to have my head stitched.

Jogging daily at Highcliffe, Hants. - 'Staving off 60'

What I liked about jogging is that it needs no planning, no partner, nothing but will power to get up and go. There is no strain, no urgency, and no competition. It is a marvellous simple sport and immensely beneficial. It protects one from heart attacks, obesity, lowers your blood pressure and keeps you alert. Getting breathless some time every day is a very good habit. You feel more alive and confident. There is a feeling of bodily well being, giving sparkle to life, taste to the palate and a boost to the morale. I recommend it for general good health, quality of life and for what we strive for, longevity. It is the stuff of life.

A short summary of the next three years to bring my life-story to a close at three score years and ten plus.

In 1989, on the 50th anniversary of World War II, my book was published and again in 1993. This created a good deal of activity for me over the next seven years. I travelled the country helping with the sales, finding myself another new experience.

I went to Scotland by train in 1991, the way I left it 50 years before. It was a nostalgic journey. The places and the people had changed. Two of my four schools attended in the 30's had disappeared and a dual carriageway and motorway now ran between the two towns of Motherwell and Hamilton. The return journey was made difficult by British Rail but because it was their fault that I missed the last train to Stroud, they sent me home by taxi from Gloucester. Who said British Rail don't care!

Also in 1991 I took a computer course at Stroud College to try and keep up with the times. It gave me an insight into the complicated subject of computer programming, data input and the practical use of software.

On an unexpected visit to Canada I flew to Toronto to take part in the annual inspection of 197 (Typhoon) Canadian Air Cadet Squadron, presented them with my squadron crest and mentioned that I had passed this way some 50 years ago on my way to flying training in Texas. They took me to Niagara Falls, to the top of the CN Tower, Toronto, and I went flying in a Cessna.

It was eight days of wonderful hospitality. Later that year I attended the celebrations of 197 Air Cadet Squadron in Plymouth. It was indeed a surprise to learn after half a century of two air cadet squadrons with the same number as that of my Typhoons. Soon after I went glider flying. Later I was delighted to make a broadcast on TV and radio on the anniversary of 'D' day.

During April I flew the Normandy Beachhead also after 50 years. We took off from Gloucester airport in a Twin Commanche aircraft belonging to John Bisco a fellow member of 80 squadron on Tempests with me in Germany 1946. Refuelling in Jersey we flew over Cherbourg, Caen, Le Harve, turning at Dieppe across the English Channel to overfly Tangmere on the way back to Gloucester. It was an unusual feeling, a painful poignant reminder of the dangerous days that are now history, looking down on the coast and countryside of France where once I dive-bombed daily. Today it looked pleasant and peaceful but it was here also where so many young lives from many countries were lost and lie buried. Sadly many names and faces flashed to mind. The 50th anniversary commemorative medal arrived soon afterwards from Caen with best wishes from Le President du Conseil Normandie.

My particular Typhoon Tale is told. Reflecting back, I realize how truly fortunate I was to have survived the War. I emerged from it without so much as a scratch and had a great time while it lasted. My Log Book shows the facts but striving to remember there is only a limited recall in my memory. With the indolence of old age comes an inchoate sense of forgetfulness!

World War II, truly a tragic event served as a positive catalyst for my life and started me on a road to happiness and prosperity. The War taught me that with the will, self-discipline, and hard work, you can conquer most things. It was a learning experience that took me from the naivety of childhood to manhood, from an ordinary life to one of hope and achievement.

It is now sixty years since World War II began. Wars are still with us, atrocities still occur. Life on this planet has become a constant struggle, a never-ending question as to who is right and who is wrong. There are few answers.

Perhaps it will all be resolved one day by something of extraordinary significance. Maybe an answer will come that will enlighten us all to a purposeful existence. A cataclysmic cosmic upheaval, a visit from outer space by an extra-terrestrial life form, a tilt of the earth's axis or a tectonic global catastrophe - one of these could determine our future. Yet before any of these may happen, and hope springs eternal, there may come the miracle of a new heavenly beginning; or the finality of the dreaded end.

Reminiscing the past 1997

The New Euro-Fighter aircraft for the New Millennium is to be named the 'TYPHOON'. This should give the Typhoon of World War Two the recognition and fame it deserves.

Epilogue

Shortly after the War ended, a most remarkable and strange thing happened to me. I awakened in the middle of the night with severe stomach cramps. Crawling from my bed in agony, I made my way in the dark on my hands and knees to the nearby Medical Centre. The doctor there quickly diagnosed the problem as an acute appendicitis and he had me transported to the main area hospital in Hannover.

The female resident surgeon decided to operate immediately. I was undressed, shaved and wheeled down a long corridor and placed on a cold operating table in a brightly lit room. While lying there, fighting unconsciousness, my entire life flashed before me in an amazing cryptic dream. It began with a long row of men in front of me, all in uniform and standing to attention. They were vaguely familiar to me. I began by walking, then in transcendental levitation, glided along before them, as if performing an inspection, acknowledging and recognising each person in turn, eye-to-eye, while I slowly passed down the line. At the end of the line a place awaited me and I was readily falling in to take my place there, when suddenly I awoke in the operating theatre to cloudy consciousness to see someone slapping my face violently and shouting, "Come on, come on, come back - oh he's one of those". The nursing staff were trying to revive and resuscitate me. They looked harassed and appeared worried for some reason. I had, they explained later, stopped breathing shortly after the surgery and efforts to revive me had been in vain that is, until my heart had started to beat again.

What no one knew was that in that short space of time, momentarily I had been dicing with death. All those people in the military queue were, in fact, my dead comrades from the War, and I had been ready to join them. It was a close call, I had almost remained there, but as in the nightmares of my youth, I again awoke to this life. Someone was still looking after me, and whoever it was, once again, was not prepared to let me cross the Great Divide forever, in any event not just yet.

My appointment in Samarra had not yet come.

James Kyle on a visit to one of the many military museums, 1989

Dedicated to all those who kept their 'Appointment in Samarra'.

ALL THE YOUNG AIRMEN

Here's to all the young airmen who flew in the wars,
Here's to all the young pilots who died,
Here's to Adolf and Werner, Alan and Sailor,
And all the others who tried.

Here's to long buried heroes who flew in the wars,
And to all their young sweethearts who cried,
Here's to young Johnnie Johnstone, Paddy and thousands
Of others who fought with both sides.

Here's to all the young fighters who fought in that summer,
Over England in thin clear blue skies,
Here's to young men and old men who saved a whole nation,
And gave their lives for that prize.

Here's to all the young nurses who stayed by their beds,
Who shed many tears when they died,
Who watched them through long nights with tender sad
mercies,
And worked so hard for their lives.

Here's to all the young airmen who flew in the wars,
Here's to all the young pilots who died,
Here's to young men and old men who saved a whole nation,
And all the others who tried.

Appendices

Aircraft Types Flown

			Year
1.	Stearman PT 18A		1941
2.	Vultee BT 13A		42
3.	NA AT6A	Wings	42
4.	Master Mk I and III		42
5.	Hurricane Mk I and IIC		42
6.	Tiger Moth		42
7.	Typhoon IA and IB	DFM	42
8.	Tempest V and II		44
9.	FW 56		45
10.	Prentice	CFS	51
11.	Harvard	QFI	51
12.	Meteor 7		51
13.	Oxford II	IRE	53
14.	Chipmunk		53
15.	Anson 19 and 21		54
16.	Provost		54
17.	Vampire TII		54
18.	Anson 21 (Navigator) and Pilot		54
19.	Lancaster (Navigator)	Small 'n'	54
20.	Mosquito		57
21.	Varsity		64

Finished Flying 1966
Appointed ATCEB 1967

Page of Log Book 1944 – showing summary of 1st operational tour.
Also letter from squadron charging 29 pints for D.F.M. Award.

Year 1944	Aircraft Type	No.	Pilot or 1st Pilot	2nd Pilot, Pupil or Passenger	Duty (Including Results and Remarks)	Single-Engine Day Dual / Pilot	Single-Engine Night Dual / Pilot	Remarks
June 2	TYPHOON	682	SELF		SQDN FORMATION			
2	TYPHOON	682	SELF		RAMROD	1:20		BURNING CAR & DAMAGED "DELAY BOMBS"
2	TYPHOON	491	SELF		NEEDS CAR TO TANGMERE	:15		
3	TYPHOON	491	SELF		TANGMERE TO NEEDS CAR	:15		
5	TYPHOON	682	SELF		AIR TEST	:10		
5	TYPHOON	682	SELF		RAMROD	1:25		BOMBING AULT — LE TREPORT AREA. LOST SGT ROSS. VERY THICK & ACCURATE LIGHT & HEAVY FLAK (AIR)
5	TYPHOON	682 JR SELF OXX			TANGMERE TO NEEDS CAR	:15		BAYEUX AREA
6	TYPHOON	682	SELF		RAMROD	1:10		"D-DAY" LOW LEVEL BOMBING OF A GHQ
7	TYPHOON	682	SELF		ARMED RECCO LARUE AREA	1:25		AT ZERO HOUR. CHANNEL A MARVELLOUS SIGHT. ATTACKED & DESTROYED GERMAN STAFF CAR WITH BOMBS & CANNONS. STRAFED DUMP & CAMP.
8	TYPHOON	682	SELF		ARMED RECCO BAYEUX-GUN	1:35		BOMBED & STRAFED ENEMY TANKS & M.T. BEHIND ENEMY LINES. CARRIED 1 LONG RANGE TANK
10	TYPHOON	549	SELF		FORMATION CAEN-FALAISE ROAD	:40		
10	TYPHOON	682	SELF		ARMED RECCO	1:00		CLOSED & STRAFED GUN POSITIONS. INTENSE FLAK (AIR)
12	TYPHOON	682	SELF		ARMED RECCO FALAISE RECONNTN AREA	1:35		STRAFED M/T TROOPS AT MESNITAM. AMY STOKES. LOST
13	TYPHOON	629	SELF		RAMROD	1:30		BOMBED & STRAFED TRUCKS. 1 DAMAGED & 1 WRECKED.
14	TYPHOON	682	SELF		RAMROD	1:10		CLOSE SUPPORT TO THE ARMY NEAR CAEN.
14	TYPHOON	682	SELF		RAMROD	1:05		CLOSE SUPPORT S OF BAYEUX. BAGS OF FLAK.
17	TYPHOON	888	SELF		RAMROD	:40		BOMBED & STRAFED BRIDGE SOUTH OF CANNES.
17	TYPHOON	688	SELF		RAMROD	1:30		RETURNED. NO CANNON. WEATHER U/S / W/C BAKER.
18	TYPHOON	752	SELF		RAMROD	:55		BOMBED BRIDGE THURY HARCOURT. LOST F. NATTON
18	TYPHOON	881	SELF		RAMROD	:16		RETURNED FRENCH COAST. WEATHER U/S

GRAND TOTAL [Cols. (1) to (10)] 611 Hrs. 30 Min.

Year 1944		Aircraft		Pilot, or 1st Pilot	2nd Pilot, Pupil or Passenger	Duty (Including Results and Remarks)
Month	Date	Type	No.			
						TOTALS BROUGHT FORWARD
June	19	Typhoon	682	Self	—	Air Test
"	22	Typhoon	682	Self	—	Ranger
"	27	Typhoon	752 C	Self	—	Fighter Escort (second)
"	29	Typhoon	804	Self	—	Air Test
"	29	Typhoon	188 V	Self	—	Armed Recco.
						SUMMARY FOR:- JUNE L. TYPHOON.
						UNIT:- 197 SQDN.
						DATE:- 30.6.44
						SIGNATURE:-
						DEFENSIVE :-
						DEFENSIVE :-
						TOTAL TYPHOON
						TOTAL OPERATIONS

GRAND TOTAL [Cols. (1) to (10)]
615 Hrs. 40 Mins.

TOTALS CARRIED FORWARD

Remarks (right side):
RETURNED A/C u/s.
BOMBING CHATEAU. GOOD RESULTS. GENERAL KILLED.
BOMBING BRIDGE AT ARGENTAN. STRAFING TRUCKS, MET.
197 SQDN. DESTROYED 6 M.E.109 + Dam 3. 2 PROBS.

Single-engine aircraft Pilot column:
100:00 / 40.00 / 40 11:50 18:00 (totals b/f)
25
10
1:25
30
1:40
23.40
20.30
324.50
187:00
180:00 / 146:50 11:50 18:00

Multi-engine aircraft / Pass. Enger:
4.30 25.20 4.00 81.00
4.20 25.20 14.00 81:00

J.K.C... P/O 8 flight
c.o. 197 SQDN.

Ramrods, Rhubarbs and Rangers

French Targets 1943/44 in order of bombing

1. TRICQUEVILLE
2. BOULOGNE
3. ABBEVILLE (10+)
4. POIX
5. CHERBOURG (10+)
6. SERQUEUX
7. FECAMP

8. C'DE LA HAQUE
9. LE HAVRE
10. LESSAY
11. BEAUMONT
12. BERNAY
13. LISIEUX
14. ANDINGHEN
15. MARTINVAAST
16. ALBERT
17. LIGESCOURT
18. BOIS DE ST SAULVE
19. LOOSTEBARVE ANDRES
20. MARQUENNITILLE
21. BEAUVOIR
22. DRIOUVILLE
23. FORET D'HESDIN
24. YVRENCH
25. MONTORQUEIL
26. ST ANDRE
27. YVRENCH BOIS CARRE
28. DIEPPE
29. LE TREPORT
30. TILLENCOURT
31. FRUGES
32. GRAND PAIQ
33. MERVIL AU VAL
34. ECLIMEAUX
35. CROISETTE
36. BOIS DE SUILHUER
37. BELLEVILLE-EN-CEUX
38. D'AILLY LE HAUT CLOCHE
39. ST LO
40. ST JOOSE AN BOIS
41. LE GROSEILLIER
42. HAMBURGES
43. KNOCKE
44. MALINES
45. DUNKIRK
46. ST POL
47. LE TOUQUET
48. AULT
49. AMIENS
50. ARRAS
51. LILLE
52. ST MALO
53. BETHUNE
54. ROUEN
55. CAEN
56. CAP D'AUTIFER
57. ARGENTAN
58. BAYEAUX
59. CABOURG
60. THURY HARCOURT
61. FALAISE
62. PARIS (not bombed)

AIR TRAFFIC CONTROL EXAMINING BOARD
VISITS - AUG 67-JUN 70

	NAME	DATE		NAME	DATE
1967			**1968**		
1.	Abingdon	Sept	13.	Scampton	Jan
2.	Kinloss	Sept	14.	Gaydon	Jan
3.	Oakington	Sept	15.	Finningley	Jan
4.	Colerne	Sept	16.	Manby	Feb
5.	Acklington	Oct	17.	St Athans	Feb
6.	Boulmer R	Oct	18.	Kemble	Feb
7.	El Adem	Oct	19.	Ternhill	Feb
8.	Bovington	Nov	20.	Eastern Radar	Feb
9.	St Mawgan	Nov	21.	Binbrook	Mar
10.	Leuchars	Nov	22.	Shawbury	Mar
11.	Gatow	Dec	23.	Stradishall	Mar
12.	Wildenrath	Dec			
24.	Chivenor	Mar	65.	Preston	Apr
25.	Cottesmore	Apr	66.	Heathrow	Apr
26.	Newton	Apr	67.	Machrihanish	May
27.	Preston	May	68.	Bruggen	May
28.	Gutersloh	May	69.	Benson	May
29.	Laarbruch	May	70.	Manston	Jun
30.	Little Rissington	May	71.	Abingdon	Jun
31.	Syerston	Jun	72.	Middle Wallop	Jun
32.	Shawbury	Jun	73.	Church Fenton	Jun
33.	Cranwell	Jun	74.	Gibralter	Jul
34.	Luqa	Jul	75.	Coningsby	Jul
35.	Bicester	Jul	76.	Ballykelly	Jul
36.	Linton-on-Ouse	Jul	77.	Thorney Island	Jul
37.	Cosford	Jul	78.	Tengah	Aug
38.	Halton	Jul	79.	Wittering	Aug
39.	Coltishall	Aug	80.	Masirah	Sept
40.	Gan	Aug	81.	Salalah .	Sept
41.	Seletar	Aug	82.	Tangmere	Oct
42.	Gutersloh	Sept	83.	Lindholme	Oct
43.	Leconfield	Sept	84.	Lyneham	Oct
44.	West Raynham	Sept	85.	Valley	Oct
45.	Thorney Island	Oct	86.	Kinloss	Nov
46.	Wroughton	Oct	87.	Linton-on-Ouse	Nov
47.	Valley	Oct	88.	Colerne	Nov
48.	Prestwick	Oct	89.	Andover	Nov
49.	Wyton	Oct	90.	Scampton	Dec
50.	Wattisham	Nov	91.	Buchan/Northern/	
51.	Marham	Nov		Flyingdale	Dec
52.	Colerne	Nov	92.	Bawdsey/Bentley	
				Priory/HQSTC	Dec
1969			93.	NATCS/MOD	Dec
53.	Finningley	Jan			
54.	Gaydon	Jan	**1970**		
55.	Fairford	Jan	94.	Leeming	Jan
56.	St Mawgan	Jan	95.	Topcliffe	Jan
57.	Leeming	Feb	96.	St Athan	Jan
58.	Eastern R	Feb	97.	Fairford	Feb
59.	Sopley	Feb	98.	Kemble	Feb
60.	Newton	Mar	99.	Waddington	Feb
61.	Akrotiri	Mar	100.	Wattisham	Mar
62.	Nicosia	Mar	101.	Binbrook	Mar
63.	Oakington	Mar	102.	St Mawgan	Mar
64.	Strubby	Apr	103.	Nicosia	Apr

RECORD OF SERVICE

UNIT	DATES From	DATES To	UNIT	DATES From	DATES To
LONDON – ST JOHNS WOOD	14/7/41	28/7/41	SOUTH CERNEY (PRENTICES) C.F.S.	17/3/57	23/5/57
No 1 I.T.W – BABBACOMBE	28/7/41	7/9/41	LITTLE RISSINGTON (JETS)	23/5/57	11/7/57
WILMSLOW	14/9/41	18/10/41	OAKINGTON (HARVARDS) (OXFORD)	12/7/57	11/12/57
MONCTON – CANADA (PT8 T/CANDA)	28/10/41	1/11/41	WELLSBOURNE MTNCS	12/2/51	5/5/53
* No 1 B.F.T.S – TEXAS (PT8 T/CANDA)	2/11/41	1/5/42	CHUMTOIS (HARVARDS)	5/5/53	11/1/54
MONCTON – CANADA	4/5/42	12/6/42	SHAWBURY (NAVIGATOR)	11/1/54	16/4/54
BOURNEMOUTH (MASTERS)	20/6/42	4/7/42	TERNHILL (PROVOSTS)	16/4/54	29/10/56
No 5 A.F.U – TERNHILL (HURRICANES)	2/7/42	8/9/42	SCHLESWIGLAND (META UTTES)	29/10/56	21/4/58
No 56 OTU – TEALING	9/9/42	1/12/42	LITTLE RISSINGTON (ITC)	21/4/58	1/3/61
* No 197 SQDN (TYPHOONS)	1/12/42	1/2/43	LUQA, MALTA (I.T.C.)	12/3/61	3/9/64
DREM, TANGMERE	1/2/43		MANBY	4/11/64	8/1/65
MANSTON, NEEDS OAR Pt.		1/4/44	STRADISHALL (VAKSITYS)	11/1/65	13/12/65
HURN, B3 FRANCE	1/4/44	31/7/44	WEST RAYNHAM (ATC)	13/12/65	31/8/67
84 G.S.U – THRUXTON	31/7/44	16/8/44	* SHAWBURY (ATC & B.)	31/8/67	22/6/70
A.D.G.B – STANMORE	16/8/44	19/8/44	SOPLEY (RADAR)	22/6/70	20/9/74
3 T.E.U – ASTON DOWN	19/8/44	16/10/44	RETIRED (BIRTHDAY)	20/9/74	(52)
26 O.T.U – WING (HURRICANES)	16/10/44	16/2/45			
84 O.T.U – DESBOROUGH	16/2/45	9/4/45			
55 O.T.U – ASTON DOWN	9/4/45	25/4/45			
83 G.S.U – DUNSFOLD	27/4/45	16/6/45			
* 80 SQDN – (TEMPESTS)	21/6/45		* ATC & B – SEE LIST.		
FASSBERG, KASTRUP,			VISITED EVERY RAF		
LUBECK, WUNSTORF			STATION (HOME &		
DEDELSTORF, SYLT			OVERSEAS.)		
GATON, MANSTON (B & B) FR					
CELLE		20/6/47			
FINNINGLEY	23/1/51	16/3/51			